STRANDS OF
A PLAIT – SINGLY

Rachel Araten

*To Rene v Meir
With love
Rachel Araten*

publishing house בית הוצאה לאור

JERUSALEM ♦ NEW YORK

Typesetting: Marzel A.S. – Jerusalem

Cover Design: Studio Paz, Jerusalem

ISBN 965 229 181 1

Edition 9 8 7 6 5 4 3 2 1

Gefen Publishing House Ltd.   Gefen Books
POB 36004   12 New Street
Jerusalem 91360 Israel   Hewlett, NY 11557 USA
972-2-538-0247   516-295-2805
E-mail: isragefen@netmedia.net.il

Printed in Israel
Send for our free catalogue

I am the creature of God,
and so is my fellowman;
my calling is in town
and his in the fields.
I go early to my work
and he to his;
he does not boast of his labor
nor I of mine.....

TALMUD

For my children and their children.

This is not a work of fiction, but neither it is a historical treatise! The episodes all took place, but for the sake of "the story," the writer has taken some liberties with time and place.

Contents

Prelude to a Homely Narrative 7

ACT ONE: Introducing the Strands   **10**

    Malka and Fräulein in a scene of scratching 10

    Esther Kordovi, a scene of prayer 11

    Vered Berlina, in a cloud of memory 15

    Malka Viene, a scene of puzzlement 19

    Lady in an armchair, briefly 22

    Ora Zemachin, a scene that is solid and restless . . 23

    Just a thought 28

    Malka prepares to go home 29

    Esther remembers history – past and present . . . 31

    Vered in a scene of toil and moil 36

    Malka listens to a tale of eating 39

    Ora in a scene of her own 42

    Malka in a scene of problem 45

    Girl in trouble of her own 49

    Vered, too, must learn to cope 52

Interlude 55

Esther in a scene of basic energy 59

Ora goes to Germany 62

Vered finds solutions 66

Malka and the Purimspiel 69

A lady at her desk 73

Ships in port 76

Scene in a café 81

Ora in a scene of distortion 84

More hurt for Vered 87

Farewell, Esther Kordovi 91

Ora and a scene of fire 95

Change of scene for Malka 100

Change for Vered, too 105

Another change for Malka 111

Ora in an unpleasant scene 115

Our strands are braided, the curtain drops 122

Prelude to a Homely Narrative

THE characters who people these pages have been called upon to tell, disjointedly – as ordinary folk do – a romantic tale, though one in which nobody falls in love. (And why "fall"? Does love not elevate?) And if they seem banal, naive or even unreal – well, so do many of us to others, especially when they don't know us.

The poetess, Ellen P. Allerton, acclaims

> "...those that do / Work that is earnest, brave and true..."

These are the kind that care least for recognition. That is just the reason why they have been picked out for the task. Haphazardly as the events which affected the course of their lives are brought before you, their tale is truly romantic in the "classic" sense of that much abused word.

A young man we know, born and bred in England, recently went on a sort of pilgrimage to modern Egypt. He asked around until one day he found himself standing in the grounds of the house where his Jewish great-grandparents and his grandparents had dwelt until the rise to power of Gamal Abdul Nasser. One could say that the young man was thrilled, but his emotions went surely deeper than that. Could you suggest a term to adequately define them? "How romantic!" one might declare. Yet, all he did was to find the place, then travel back to his usual domicile.

The perhaps trite events of the simple souls we shall get to know reveal a tale of homecoming because of their need to come and to stay. More than that, their tale takes place during the rebuilding of their ancient, neglected home; it shows the energy, fired by loving devotion as much as by need, that is invested in the labor; and at last the gates of HOME are opened. And opened wide, at that, offering permanent hospitality to the entire, extended family of Jews, from wherever its members come, whatever mental equipment they will have acquired from previous surroundings, of whatever hue their skin may be. Nor will they need to leave again.

> But what about the cost? The cost in pain – mental no
> less than physical, the cost in tears, aggravation,
> heartache?

Thriving and modern as this "young" country may appear to tourists and newcomers, the task has never been easy, never been without its periods of torment, the greater torment that leaves a person stunned, and the lesser torments that frustrate simpler souls to the point of screaming.

What were they like, these unknowns who toiled and passed on, or who sat back in eventual exhaustion until their time came?

We can tell the story of very few, no more than can be counted on the fingers of a single hand. For in this technological era of haste and hustle, where is the reader who would wade through the necessary hundreds of thousands of pages? But our few are fairly typical, at least of half of the population.

However, if we claim that their narrative is romantic, let us try to give it something of a dramatic flavor, too.

Picture a forest. Each tree in the forest, in copse, grove and wood, has its own roots in its patch of soil. So long as no sickness attacks them, the trees grow thick, tall and sturdy. When the winds are storm-laden, the topmost branches may entangle with those of nearby trees. But down beneath the topsoil, every tree has its own roots. Ablaze with light as the sun may be, the entangled boughs keep the forest dark and the darkness may provide shelter of sorts in times of need.

Nevertheless, trees are individual growths. And even in the seasonal fall, when they appear to lose their vitality with their leaves, yet are the trees alive. Their roots furnish them with the sustenance that will renew their greening.

Thus, too, is it with the Jewish nation. Some may shrink when the thunder rolls, may flinch at the flash of lightning. And, at times, during the storms of life, some of us take paths which may interlace us into a thickly coiled braid; others may let themselves be hurled, singly and unprotesting, into the density of the thoughtless, unquiet mob. Either path presents its problems.

But we humans can think. We can recollect. Such skills should be considered wondrous. Yet, strangely enough, each one of us is no more significant than a grain of sand – or, if you prefer, if it sounds kindlier to your consciousness, than a single strand of a plait of human hair.

Is it not so? Would you remind us that

"All the world's a stage..."?

Then let us imagine ourselves in a kind of theater where we sit back and watch the wind blowing each fine strand of hair singly in one or another direction.

ACT ONE

Introducing the Strands

Malka and Fräulein in a scene of scratching

"Fräulein," boomed a deep voice from the top of the staircase, "Fräulein, you must not scratch!"

The Fräulein looked up. For two whole weeks a port strike had kept in Marseilles the boat that at last had brought her to Haifa. She had spent the fortnight in a nearby French village where the mosquitoes had feasted on her face, her arms, her legs, wherever they found a patch of uncovered skin. Finally at sea, the itching had abated somewhat, but after some weeks in the dry heat of the late Palestine summer, heavily breathed on by the harsh east wind, new watery blobs were again tormenting her skin. When she thought herself alone, she scratched.

The owner of the booming voice now came down the stairs and examined the blisters.

"Every newcomer gets one of three afflictions, if not all," she declared, "but you are lucky, you have the least of the three."

"Three afflictions?" gasped the newcomer.

"There is malaria, though less than there used to be. Then there is poppadacha, but what you have is harara."

The voice was authoritative, its accent Viennese. It belonged to a tall, Junoesque matron who introduced herself as Malka. The kindness in her eyes belied the assertiveness in her tone. The Fräulein was puzzled:

"Poppadacha? Harara? I never heard such names. What are they?" She would later, she thought, look them up in her medical dictionary, but the voice boomed out again, this time in laughter:

"Doctors use other names, Latin or Greek. Then they seem worse, as though they were heavy diseases. But poppadacha is only a digestive matter; the stomach has to get used to different foods. Harara comes from the heat, your skin can't take it yet. But you may not scratch or you will get wounds that may turn nasty. Come, I will bathe the blisters for you."

Poppadacha was not to be found in her dictionary, but the young girl heard the term often enough for familiarity, and she never did get malaria. D.D.T. was brought into the country around that time and proved a blessing in helping to rid the country of its mosquitoes. The harara cleared up.

* * *

Esther Kordovi, a scene of prayer

Once upon a time (such a lovely, old-fashioned phrase, but this is the old-fashioned part of our narrative), Jews had found in British Singapore a comfortable place for settling – at least until some untoward occurrence would require a fresh peregrination. Those Jews were well aware that moving on was a matter of course every few generations. In many countries one or more members of a family had remained behind, perhaps to look after whatever remained of property that needed attention, or perhaps had been reluctant to move on, at whatever cost the staying necessitated. Hiding? Baptism? Well, moving to strange places wasn't that easy, either!

In Singapore, City of the Lion, the newest generation of a particular family had no reason to be dissatisfied with their predecessors' choice. So long as this small Malaysian city remained a British Crown Colony of the Straits Settlement, nothing in the laws of Judaism the Kordovi family so lovingly adhered to would prevent them from becoming honorable citizens. In fact, they became honored citizens, prospering mightily in the world of commerce so easily afforded by the Port of Singapore, whence the great ships took and brought, in transit, the produce of a toiling world.

So for a great many decades the Kordovis enjoyed prosperity and freedom of worship. When their offspring grew to adolescence the parents sent them to study at the great universities of Britain. Life in England pleased the young Kordovis. In time, they found mates and settled there. Back in Singapore life took its usual course: The parents, Benedict and Esther, had each other. They had their fine home, its colonial style of life with a staff of servants attending to their every need; their circle of friends afforded them a pleasant social life and, of course, every ship would bring the affectionate newsy letters that gave them a picture of their children's lives all those miles away.

Till Benedict fell ill. There was but a brief spell of painful treatment and then the finality of the funeral.

Esther Kordovi found herself pondering hard choices. What was there now for her to do? There had been a worry at the back of her mind, a worry she had refrained from mentioning to her husband during those last weeks, but she could not now stop herself from brooding over it: The newspapers, she felt, were making too much of that Austrian house painter or whatever he was, and his cheap and ugly rhetoric. She could not avoid the thought that, should serious trouble erupt, it would not be confined to Europe. That Austrian creature seemed to be attracting more sympathy in Japan, her part of the world, than wisdom and integrity should have advised.

It was her custom to begin her day with prayer. Watch her! She reads the Hebrew carefully and correctly, with respect. Then she turns to the English translation on the opposite page. She knows it by heart, it is the knowledge of a lifetime, but she finds it important always to make sure she has understood her prayers properly. Especially now, when faith in the God of her Fathers is all of true value that, without her husband, is left to her. Re-reading the stately, ancient phrases, she recalls some words of a prayer that Benedict had once read aloud to her with great emphasis. She seemed to recall that the prayer had been specially composed for one of her nation's too frequent encounters with disaster. Esther, in her present trouble, cannot recall the exact occasion; was it written at the time of a pogrom? A blood libel? Had it been intended to offer hope to the thousands of Jews at starvation point across the shtetls of the Pale of Settlement? Or was it during Stalin's murderous rule?

It makes no matter! The point is that the words, or part of them, have taken hold of her memory. Esther sees the print, she feels the words in her soul.* Now in her lonely, prayerful hour, they come back to her with the forcefulness of an omen:

> "Rock and Redeemer of Israel... redeem our suffering brethren... gather in the scattered children of Israel, and restore them to the Land of Israel..."

Her mind is robbed of any other idea – but a hard thought intrudes: Does she really wish to leave Singapore? Not visit Benedict's grave again? That is a painful thought, conscience-touching. Something that Jews don't do.

But then, her husband's family, the Kordovis, like her own, the Levys – how often over the centuries had they all been forced, mostly at short notice, to take up and go, just leave and roam to find some other clime, to adjust hastily to different scenes, to unwonted conditions of life! Had it been easy to learn another tongue? Had it been pleasant to have strangers smile at their clumsy accent and faulty idiom? Had it been so simple to have to find another way of earning their bread, of getting used to strange foods? And, hardest of all, there had always been the double

---

* The author has allowed herself "poetic license," as to date; the Special Prayer was composed in 1971 by Ashkenazi Chief Rabbi Isser Yehuda Unterman.

problem of sheltering their children from harm and hurt while keeping them in the cultural path of their Jewish forebears.

All these details pass through Mrs. Kordovi's mind as she stands there with her prayer book in hand. A voice inside her declares firmly: Enough!

She would have to leave Benedict's grave unvisited, unattended. The ancient hallowed homeland of her people was, she knew, being rebuilt with energy and great love, with hope in a venture that must bear fruit.

Titus was long no more than a skeleton in the ground. The mighty Rome that had conquered Judea existed only in print. And how many read it? Why had the Jews waited so long? There is no real answer to that question, but now the immediate future was at stake. Thinking of Japan and of the contents of the newspapers she pored over mornings, she knew there was only one way ahead.

She must go to her real homeland. Esther Kordovi has money, energy, enthusiasm and – God help her – the freedom now to choose her own road.

She would build herself a small house out there, a house with a garden. She would plant flowers and trees. Lonely? She was no youngster but a middle-aged woman. Would loneliness be a harsh burden? But her human mind, she tells herself, will endow her trees with the quality of life. They would nod to her outside her window. They would bid her "Good morning" when she awoke, and "Good night" when she drew her curtains at dusk.

When the wind blows, trees bend back and forth – as if praying. Her trees would pray with her on sad, wintry days as the gusty winds would blow them in all directions.

"I shall build my house on a hilltop," Esther promises herself; and in the environment of nature she would herself create, she would find friendliness in her widowhood.

**

Vered Berlina, in a cloud of memory

Looked at from years into the future, Vered's was a strange kind of home, one that seemed inflexibly to demand a capital H. The single photograph that Vered had kept when she needed so hurriedly to pack showed her as an exquisitely pretty girl. In those days a girl ready for marriage was referred to, in the heaviness of the German tongue, as a *Backfisch*; though she spoke no other language, Vered found this a silly, even an insulting word. A fish ready to be baked?

Nowhere else would such a metaphor have been applied to her: An impish look laughed out of her heart-shaped face, but those blue-gray eyes had a clean, straightforward glance, as well. Thick, curly dark hair rebelled against the command to lie smoothly around her head; no matter how often the brush was applied, it was used in vain, despite her grandmother's disapproval of such an untidy head.

In the "Great War" (you recall the war that was to end all wars?), Vered's father, serving his land and Kaiser, was killed in battle. Then an epidemic ran through the town and, like a press-gang, snatched away her mother. The orphaned infant was taken to her grandmother's house in Stuttgart, where a trained nanny was put in charge of her.

Stuttgart, capital city of the German province of Württemberg, was (still is, probably) a beautiful city, owing to its hilly environment and the greenness of its countryside – at least in summer. The smells of the farming suburbs in the plain wafted upwards, to be sniffed in pleasure. It was a city of great culture, famous for its annual Book Fair, its theaters, its concert halls. Every public building, whatever its purpose, had its own impressive architecture. But what the small Vered chiefly delighted in was gazing down from a hilltop at the view below. Her sturdy, country-bred nanny, taking the child on a rare visit to her own farming family, would tell the youngster:

"Can you smell the cows? Breathe in that air, it is good for the lungs." How often Vered was laughed at for repeating that; all her life she insisted that "the smell of cows was good for the lungs."

Many years later, in 1933, when her home (with a small h) was but a white, square, flat-faced dwelling sticking up out of acres of yellow sand, Vered had occasion to visit Haifa. Looking down from Mount Carmel on Haifa's fairyland scenery, Vered, still petite, her thick, curly hair now silvering, declared fervently:

"Ah, here, if we could have settled here on the Carmel, with a cow or two, I could have lost my homesickness."

In her grandmother's house, the one with the capital H, she was brought up to correct behavior, impeccable manners, an inflexible sense of integrity. She was also taught to curtsy gravely to her elders and to guests. In those later years, as her feet sank, step by heavy step, into the sand of the Holy Land's early settlement, her laughter could still bubble forth:

"How lucky we don't need to curtsy here! (*Hier muss man keine Knickse machen!*) We would sink into the sand if we had to."

If distant in manner, as behooves an old lady in a house with a capital H, her grandmother still treated her with the conscientious kindness due to her dead son's only child. Early on, the small Vered came to understand that she had always to ensure for herself her grandmother's approval. The rules were strict.

Once a year, fortunately, everyone had a birthday. For eleven long obedient months the child waited for this event. As the final month of her year crept on, the little one felt the excitement growing in her; she fought hard to keep it under control. She dared not let it become visible, lest some fault of decorum requiring punishment be revealed. Instinctively, from infancy, Vered knew that if only she could keep this mounting tension from betraying her, there would, on the great day, be a small package on her breakfast plate. And in the afternoon there would be creamcake for tea! That once-a-year creamcake left its taste on her palate right into old age. No delicacy ever tasted quite like that.

In Israel her hair was still unruly despite its silvering sheen. The impish look vanished into the closet of life's experience. Though everything about her spoke of former opulence, she never talked aloud about "the good old days." She never used the word "grandmother," nor even in German fashion did she speak of her "Oma." It was always "My Old Lady" (*Meine Alte Dame*) – in capital letters.

Marriage had taken her from Stuttgart and its discipline to Berlin, where, according to old acquaintances, her home had been "like a palace." She herself never mentioned it. She employed a housemaid and later, when her children, a boy and then a girl, were born, she engaged a nanny, too. But the nanny was often left at home with some sewing or mending. The great enjoyment of Vered's life at that time was walking out with her little ones to the zoo, along a lane leafed in by lime trees, or to a public garden where the greensward was soothing and the flowered borders glorious. The evenings afforded her the music she loved at concerts or opera in her husband's company.

Children did, of course, need to behave properly, especially so that once a year, until the death of "My Old Lady," she could take them down to Stuttgart to visit. But she herself had been too well disciplined to explode in harshness at any little naughtiness; her two children had a gentle mother. Life moved along smoothly, until that day in 1933 when her husband came home all bruised and beaten up and told her:

"Quick, pack a bag and get the children ready; we must leave at once."

Unlike the widow in Singapore, they had taken little notice of the menacing rumblings, had heeded no warnings. Perhaps, they had told themselves, there would be a pogrom now and then, as there had been a generation back in the Pale of Settlement. That was why grandfather had left his East European hamlet and had come to Berlin. Jews were used to pogroms. Very nasty for some days, then passing. True, a pogrom left much damage behind – but never had they prepared their minds for the possibility that here, in Goethe's cultured land, in the civilized world they had so admired and so devotedly served, they would be rejected. It never entered their minds that after such long acquaintance, such real patriotism, this solid place they called "home" would complacently cooperate in trying to obliterate them, merely because they were Jews.

But Vered, her husband and children were fortunate: They got away in time. They could build a new life. "Build" quite literally.

All those elegant clothes – the velvet toque with its eye-veil, the cape of soft fur, the tailored suits and costumes – khaki shorts and loose tops replaced them. In the heat of the Palestine summer, such baggy clothes were more comfortable for the task of breaking stony ground, for leaching the salt out of sandy soil, for digging, planting and sowing, for preparing chicken feed, for scrubbing tiled floors, for laundering, for brushing the dust out of the wire netting covering windows, that in the pre-D.D.T. days kept the flies and mosquitoes at bay in some measure.

What a catalog of chores for this long, narrow strip of barren land!

There is no nanny, no housemaid. Certainly, there is no greensward, no glorious flowers, there is scarcely a tree to be seen.

On rare occasions, very rare, Vered would look upward and say:

"What a lovely color the sky is! It must be something to wear a silk dress in that shade of blue."

But who had time to recall what had been left behind in that palatial Berlin home?

And what did it matter?

* * *

Malka Viene, a scene of puzzlement

In a Viennese home, tall, majestic Malka was reading a letter for the third or fourth time. A year or so earlier, her daughter had gone to Tel Aviv with her Maccabi sports group for the first Jewish "Olympic" games that took place in 1932. Jews and sports? Jews competing in such events? That was unusual, exciting even. Malka had consented somewhat reluctantly, finally agreeing with her husband that no real harm could come of letting the girl have her way; after all, she was nineteen years old. The games were long over, but the lass was still in Tel Aviv. And now she had written that she intended to stay there. She would not be returning to Vienna.

Malka made herself a cup of coffee. This letter needed thinking out before her husband and son came home for the evening meal. She had to keep calm. She admitted to herself that she was rather an autocratic mother, perhaps too much so. But then, one needed to be careful with girls, surely? Had she been so wise in agreeing to the trip? But how could she have imagined that her daughter would not want to come back home?

Certainly, Palestine was the Holy Land, the birthplace of the Jewish nation. And they, the family, were Jews. All very well, but as far as she knew, Palestine was not really an inhabited place. She considered Herzl as something of a visionary, unrealistic. Of course, she was proud of his connection with Vienna and the respect accorded him; such a handsome man! But that all Jews should get up, leave their homes and go out to live in the Holy Land? What a strange idea!

Her daughter's letters had given her a vivid impression of a land entirely neglected, bare and barren. Her beautiful daughter, a highly intelligent girl, so much had been invested in her schooling. Why on earth should she want to settle in such an undeveloped country, a place without any modern amenities?

Of course, the family was always aware of their Jewishness, there was enough anti-Semitism in Austria, had been for years and years, to keep them aware. The Hebrew prayer book with its

German translation had, on solemn occasions, been taken out of its embroidered velvet cover. The extended family always gathered for Jewish Holy Days and traditional ceremonies. And a few coins were regularly dropped into "the little blue box" on the kitchen shelf.

For the rest, they considered themselves no more Jewish than Viennese.

Yet her fun-loving, musical daughter was now intent on giving up the concerts and operas, the elegance, the gaiety, the delightful Wienerwald, the Prater with its *Riesenrad* (huge ferris wheel) – everything that made Vienna the alluring city it was. Why? Malka sipped her coffee slowly. She would find the answer before she got to the bottom of the cup.

Her conclusion was natural: "There must be a young man in the matter," said her mother's heart. This was serious. She would have to see for herself. Young girls set free from parental authority were often a bit flighty. So, she decided, for a few weeks husband and son would manage without her; she would have no argument about it.

Her bag was packed, her ship's ticket purchased before they had convinced themselves that she truly meant to travel.

Malka herself could scarcely believe it when, some days later, she found herself sitting on her suitcase in the port of Haifa, looking at the faces of passersby. Having notified no one of her arrival, no one could be expected to wait for her. She had the address of a relative written on the back of an envelope, and this she held out to anyone passing, asking for instructions on how to get there.

The reply was brief: *"Lo yodéa."* (Hebrew for: "don't know.") From the body language, the shoulder shrug, the shake of the head, Malka understood that *"Lo yodéa"* meant "Not Jewish." *"Yodéa"* sounded to her like "Jude" – Jew. And no matter how many people she asked, she got the same response. She tried to make her Viennese German sound like Yiddish, but it didn't help.

"No Jews here?" she asked herself. How could that be? For Heaven's sake, what could have gotten into her daughter's mind?

And then she told herself that, of course, Jews would not be port laborers; they would work in a town, in shops or offices. Finally she found a taxi, the driver knew the address, and she came to the home of her relatives. In later years she laughed at herself, but on that day, she gave them no chance to laugh at her but burst out with the question:

"How come that there are hardly any Jews here? Not a single one down near the port. And how is it possible that no one knows where a street is in such a small place?"

They tried to calm her:

"There are plenty of Jews here," she was assured, "but the houses are built one by one. When there is quite a row of them, one can call it a street. But then it is a new street, there has to be a meeting of the local council. Names are suggested and the matter has to be argued out. Agreement on such things is not always unanimous. And by the time a name is agreed upon, new houses nearby will be going up to form a new row. You can't expect everyone to know every line of houses that gets put up – there's building going on everywhere, it is part of the daily scene."

Malka's pride kept her from admitting that she really didn't know what they were talking about. Cities had streets and streets had names, even if the place was, as she had thought, uninhabited. She would not reveal that "building the Land" had not been understood as being literally so, she had thought it a kind of slogan for the encouragement of Zionist theory. Building actually meant digging foundations, pouring concrete into molds, putting brick on brick?

"What had the place looked like then?" she wondered, recalling her daughter's letters, "had it really been bare, just rough ground?"

And with a sudden, unwonted rush of pride, Malka told herself:

"We Jews, we little *Yidden*, built this up ourselves? From nothing?" She wished at that moment that she could bring her

Gentile neighbors from Vienna and show them what Jews could do.

To the Fräulein who arrived three years later, scratching blisters, Malka would boast of how she had learnt her first two words of Hebrew – *"Lo yodéa"* – within half an hour of her arrival. She did not mention that she had found it hard to learn much more. In fact, it had been her intention to return to Vienna, so why need she have bothered?

* *
*

Lady in an armchair, briefly

So! She had been a Fräulein. Her German-English dictionary (why had she brought so many lexicons with her?) told her the term implied a young girl of good ʿfamily. No argument about that! Moreover, in Malka's softly-vowelled Viennese German, the word had sounded like a caress, despite the boomingly deep voice that used it. Malka made "Fräulein" sound so much more "status-like" than the Hebrew *"Metapelet,"* and certainly less off-putting than the English "governess," which is what she was. She had been perfectly content to answer to "Fräulein" when called.

Funny how the appellation had stuck, hardly anyone seemed to know or use her real name.

But as time passed, slowly as the years moved on, and so speedily as they had gone, she became aware of herself really becoming nameless, an old non-person in this land of the young. Sometimes the thought was painful. The women of her generation in their time had done as much as any man in the rebuilding, had taken in their stride the hard life they had found in this strip of sand, thorns and thistles.

And now, old and tired, they belonged to no one, were namelessly unrecognized. But maybe it didn't really matter? Many people passed during their lifetimes out of the hurly-burly of this human rush. They may even have merited a period of non-personhood, a time for looking on before closing their eyes.

She, too, would look on; more probably she would look back. From the distance of time some comprehension may have been attained.

Ora Zemachin, a scene that is solid and restless

"Once upon a time" (that lovely phrase again), people spoke of a non-existent wonder: the time machine; it was supposed to show any period of history one might want to see or live in.

In our era of electronic marvels, we can bring back the past with a real instrument: the remote control. We hold it out, a longish, black bar of a thing, press one of its raised numbers, and living pictures come through the walls into our rooms. And often, when "someone" (in a boardroom? discussing?) decides the nation should be reminded of an event, it is the dead who come to life! Famous folk, long in their graves, are now seen and heard, getting into cars, making speeches, singing songs – just as though they really were still around. "Lest we forget." There is too much that should not be forgotten, but the viewers have little say in the matter, they are not asked if or what they wish to relive.

And yet, the greater power is theirs: They have merely to switch off. The screen goes blank, the past has vanished.

Although it hardly crossed her mind that she was "exercising power," Leonora would often switch off when a TV program, or even a book, failed to hold her interest. The irony in this was that she herself possessed a veritable store of memories that should be on record for their part in our people's modern formation. But it needed switching on. This was done by the nameless Fräulein with whom Leonora had become acquainted almost a lifetime ago. Her friend asked, and, reluctantly or not, Leonora made use of her private remote control to open her own Pandora's box. Actually, she was not called Leonora. She disliked the lengthiness of the name and wondered how her East European Yiddish-speaking parents had given her such an English name. Perhaps it was her older siblings who had made the choice. She insisted on being known by just the last three letters: Ora. That sounded simple; she disliked anything "fancy-shmancy" – which was nothing to be surprised at, once one had learnt her "down-to-earth" history.

The name turned out to be a strangely good idea when, in 1951, she came to live in Israel, for Ora, in Hebrew, means "light." Ora was just sixteen when Germany marched into Poland, and England declared war. Like so many youngsters of that time, she was evacuated to a country village. But nothing much was happening, the newspapers spoke of a "phony" war, and after a year or so, Ora returned to London.

There she found things rather different: For one thing, her home was no longer crowded with so many siblings; then it seemed to her new awareness that her parents were more bewildered than she remembered, not understanding, if they had ever before, just what was happening, or even what life was about. There was little she could do for them, and she opted to move in with her elder sister who had rented a small flat above a shop in one of London's long, busy High Streets.

It was a broad thoroughfare, lined along both sides with the flashily decorated windows of shops that gave strolling window-shoppers no hint of the shabby old houses built in deadly monotonous rows branching out behind it.

Trams and trolley-buses rumbled along at all hours. Just across the road, folk would be lining up, afternoons and evenings, outside the cinema, a seemingly glamorous place bearing the grand name "The Regal." The cinema-goers were equipped "for the flicks" with bags of peanuts or, in summer, with a brown paper bag of cherries purchased from the nearby fruitstall.

Farther along the road was the local Town Hall, a surprisingly imposing edifice for this part of London. One wing of the building had been designed as a concert hall and here, too, people would queue up for tickets to the latest "Revue," a popular cockney entertainment. The program seldom differed: On stage, rows of girls in glittering apparel would swirl and twirl in rhythm with music that, compared with the modern, physically provoking rowdiness of sound, could be judged as gentle, despite its rhythmic beat. Then there were singers – men with top hats always slightly askew. They would also tell jokes, and their burlesque would be interspersed with topical witticisms and satire that evoked roars of appreciative laughter from the working-class audience. The Finale, generally a modest imitation of can-can kicks, skirts, thighs and legginess, would send viewers home in right good humor. "A pint or two" at the pub on the corner would, as likely as not, alter the mood somewhat.

Over the way, almost opposite the Town Hall, was the Public Library, again a building of modest, yet impressive architecture. To belong, one only needed to present a taxpayer's guarantee. The library provided a space of calm, in contrast to the rumbling, busy scene outside its walls. Here, on dull days during weekends and school holidays, pairs of "inseparable" friends "doing" French at their Secondary School would pore over what was to them the nonsense of Rabelais, suppressing their giggles to the point of stomach ache. A library Reading Room was one of the rare places in Britain where the word "Forbidden" could be found; applied to noise, it was a word to be respected.

The fairly empty pockets of most parents in the neighborhood, especially the pockets of Jewish immigrants, sent their adolescents to this free library, rather than to the Regal or the Revue. The youngsters, naturally, resented the poverty that limited them to this world of print, indifferent to or unaware of its enormous advantages.

In any case, it was hardly likely that Ora's parents could or would go to either place of amusement. And eventually the phony war put off its disguise to become a fearsome, continuous familiarity. Ora came to a quick decision: She left London and joined the Land Army. She wanted, she said, to escape the bombs falling on the town.

One may hazard a guess that the memory of the first evacuation had filled her with a sense of green quietude, of the spaciousness so congenial to her nature. The tiny flat, the noise of the busy, crowded street – it all gave her the feeling of being hemmed in. She yearned for something else without knowing just what; she told herself it was freedom she craved. But who can define the meaning of the word? Who does not want "freedom" – but from what?

"Well, but what of your Jewishness?" she was asked. The Nazis had been in power for some years; had that meant anything to her?

"Of course, we knew we were a Jewish family," Ora admitted, "but we had little notion of what that meant. My feeling was that I was carrying this Jewishness around like a heavy sack, but I never knew why the sack was heavy."

It was easy to see the origin of her metaphor. Ora's parents had come to Britain from their East European hamlet, firm in the knowledge that "Torah learning is the finest earning." It was bewildering to discover that, although the Bible was the country's "best-seller," the Torah learning could neither feed nor clothe the growing family, nor could it pay the rent.

Still, her father, a strong, well-built man, had no trouble lugging a heavy sackful of trinkets and oddments that were easily peddled in the countryside. The Gentile villagers soon came to recognize this good-natured Jew as an honest, well-meaning soul. Even if his English was scarcely intelligible as such, he was able for a time to make a living.

But then an accident or illness, perhaps a slight stroke – one did not confide in children in those days, so they never knew just what had happened – left him incoherent for the rest of his life. This put a stop to even the tenuous contact he had ever had with his English-born, English-educated offspring. Probably he remained unaware that they had gotten out of attending Hebrew classes as soon as they realized there was nothing he could do about it. The old man could have told his children at length and with profound understanding about the work of the great Kabbalist, Isaac Lurie of Safed, and they could have told him with equally full understanding about Luria, the Moor who commanded the Forces of Florence, as narrated by Robert Browning in his dramatic poem. But just as their father could not relate to this, neither would they have found interest in the former.

During the days of his coherence, he had often impressed on his family, or tried to, that they came from a line of famous, important rabbis. The adolescents dismissed this as mere bragging, the attempt of a man who could hardly make a living to arouse and hold his sons' respect. But their home had scarce comfort, they were hard-put to hold their own with their schoolmates. What was the point of talk about belonging to famous rabbis?

What these youngsters did not know was that their surname was no mere Yiddish concoction difficult to pronounce, strange to English ears. The name was an acronym, the initials of a respected scholarly family who lived during the Middle Ages. Some of its members had left to posterity written results of deeply philosophical studies of Judaism. After the expulsion of Jews from Spain, one of the family found temporary asylum in Majorca, where he composed a treatise refuting the value of Christianity. After this he had to take his family from that island to toil across strange lands, driven from place to place by Jew-hating actions and attitudes.

Had one of the family gotten himself to Singapore? Had he any connection with the Kordovis? We do not know, but it is surely possible.

"Pedigree" declares an old adage, "pedigree lies in the cemetery!" But what difference would knowledge of this authentic lineage have made to Ora and her siblings? Pride is neither edible nor saleable. Throughout her youth Ora had thought along these lines, but after her wartime experiences and after many years of life in Israel, she declared, as surprisingly to herself, probably, as to her listener:

"Well, actually, pride in one's forebears can serve as a standard to emulate and try to reach."

* *
*

Just a thought

More than a century ago, William Makepeace Thackeray, the English writer of Vanity Fair fame, made a rather unusual declaration:

"Some philosophers," he said, "get their wisdom with deep thought and out of ponderous libraries. I pick up my small crumbs of cogitation at a dinner table; or from Mrs. Mary and Miss Louise as they are prattling over their five o'clock tea."

With Lewis Carroll's permission, a cat may look at a king. Just so may any humble creature take example from a greater; that is why any "small crumbs of cogitation" in this narrative are taken from the Jewish-Israeli likes of "Miss Louise and Mrs. Mary." In Israel, however, true relaxation is a rare luxury, life here being too often full of tension. Nor would we claim that there is much "prattling" over afternoon tea or coffee. Discussion will focus mostly on the problems of the country, too often leading to heated arguments that result in anything but relaxation. If we were sensible and wanted to have quietude at least in our private lives, we would drink our tea or coffee in perfect silence!

But who would expect such an impossibility?

"Cogitation" is a burdensome word – but let us borrow a small crumb of thought from one of our own: from the Jewish philosopher Hermann Cohen who, in 1918, was emphatic in his belief that

> *"Everything heroic in man is insignificant and perishable, and all his wisdom and virtues unable to stand the final test unless they are the fruits of*

> *humility. In this there is no exception – neither for any man, any people or any age..."*

Who are we to argue with that? Let us watch our own "Mrs. Mary and Miss Louise" along their way – and see.

Malka prepares to go home

Her mother's heart had informed her correctly: Malka's daughter had fallen in love and would live in Tel Aviv after marriage. The young man himself had also come from Vienna with the Maccabi sports group, and Malka wondered at herself for having been so unsuspecting. However, she was pleased with her daughter's choice and decided she could now return to her home in Vienna with a quiet mind.

Not for a minute did Malka think about the meaning of that word "home" during that late autumn of 1932. Towards the end of November she took the bus from Tel Aviv to Haifa, where the ship bound for Trieste would shortly arrive in port. But she found her relatives there crowding around the wireless set. No one spoke of a "radio" in those days. As November passed and December's days began to roll off the calendar, the mood of foreboding deepened: Hitler became Chancellor of Germany.

If not erudite, Malka was certainly an intelligent woman.

"The knave will take over Austria," she foresaw. It would be unwise to go back just now. She must wait awhile and see how things turned out. If the situation worsened, her husband and son could join her in Haifa, a city she preferred to Tel Aviv.

Jews had been living quite comfortably in Vienna, comparatively speaking. They enjoyed a degree of assimilation that made them feel Austrian; and yet they also liked the sense of particularity that the synagogue services gave them on those "special occasions," and certainly they enjoyed participating in the traditional meals with fellow Jews, chanting familiar, if unintelligible hymns that, melodiously, aroused emotional sentimentality. They were nonetheless aware of the anti-

Semitism, past and present, which told them that their formal Austrian citizenship would not protect them when waves of Jew-hatred overwhelmed their Gentile compatriots. They knew perfectly well that if a Jew had ever been ambitious, conversion to Christianity was a necessity, especially for obtaining academic positions.* Austria was a Catholic country and the Hapsburgs intended to keep it so. There had been some nine thousand conversions between the years 1868 – 1903. In their own hearts, Jews resented this phenomenon but understood the reason for it.

Hitler's hostility, however, was not towards Judaism as a religion. It was the nation of Jews he rejected. This was clearly expressed for him by the Chairman of the Christian Social Party, Edmund Czernak (himself no Austrian, but a Slav) who stated openly that

> "...in our national culture Jews cannot be allowed to have any say except as guests... they have their real homeland in Palestine..."

Majestic Malka, sitting erectly silent near the wireless set, decided to remain in Haifa for the time being. She needed no book-learning to convince herself of the wisdom of her resolve.

By March 1933, as many Jews as could manage to cross a border were fleeing Nazi terror to any place that would let them in. But her husband and son delayed until it was too late. The young man had a girl friend, while her husband had a business that required attention. And furniture had to be stored or disposed of – did his wife expect a responsible man to simply lock the door and take ship?

One cannot stay with relatives indefinitely. With her good looks, commanding personality, her quick understanding and especially her warmth and willingness, our Majestic Malka soon found herself a job. She was so admiringly cooperative with the building of the raw land, became so devoted to her work, that Vienna might have been a thousand light years away. Its charm,

---

* *Vienna and its Jews,* by Pr. Berkley

its amusements, its special elegance – all of it took on the hue of superficiality.

Except for the letters that came at intervals:

"I have gotten married, Mama," her son wrote.

A later letter bore an enclosure: "Mama, here is a photo of my wife and son. You are a grandma!"

But when would she be able to fondle the baby? When would she take him out in the carriage, wearing a little woolen suit of her own knitting, and show the child proudly to family and friends?

Finally, there came a letter bearing a cry of despair:

"Mama, they took them away. My lovely wife, my beautiful little son. Mama, what will happen to them?"

No more letters came. "They" came for him and his father.

Malka, how did you get through the years with that pain gnawing at you?

* * *

Esther remembers history – past and present

The climate of Singapore was hot and exceedingly humid. Esther Kordovi, arriving at her destination before the outbreak of war, found the air of the coastal plain too damp for her liking, and that of Jerusalem too dry, especially when south-easterly winds breathed so heavily over the city. She decided to settle in Safed. Its narrow old streets gave her the feeling of Jewish closeness.

Besides, in this quaint little place she found special meaningfulness, it strengthened her passion for history.

"Whatever took place yesterday, or last week or last year," she was fond of saying, "has had its influence on what is happening now."

1492 is the very familiar date of the Expulsion of the Jews from Spain. Ironically, it was also the year when Columbus set out to discover a new route to India, and instead came to the New World that centuries later gave shelter to Jews fleeing from the Old one. In that same year of 1492, Spain finally rid itself of the Moors who had dominated so much of that country since their invasion of it in 711.

Mrs. Kordovi associated these events with greed, power-lust and worse: with bigotry, a fanatical lack of tolerance. She had so often thought about those Jews driven from their homes, deprived of their livelihoods, merely because they refused to abjure their ancient faith. She tried to picture the scene of their leaving, wondering how close to truth was the description sketched out in 1883 – almost four hundred years later – by Emma Lazarus:

> "The halt, the blind, are amid the train. Sturdy pack-horses laboriously drag the tented wagons wherein lie the sick athirst with fever.
>
> "The panting mules are urged forward by spur and goad; stuffed are the heavy saddle-bags with the wreckage of ruined homes.
>
> "...Oh, the weary march! oh, the uptorn roots of home; oh, the blankness of the receding goal!...."*

Were they really permitted to take mules and pack-horses? The women, the small children – did they walk, day by day, for miles at a time? How did they manage to get food? What about clothing? How did they keep it and themselves clean?

Yes, these were all long ago matters, but Esther Kordovi could not keep her thoughts away from them for long, because her own ancestors, like her husband's, had been part of that horde of fugitives, or did they call them refugees? Or did they answer to some other designation?

She could not form a clear picture in her mind of that kind of exodus; and any "time machine" or "remote control" reconstruction could be based only on imagination.

---

* Excerpt from "The Exodus," by Emma Lazarus

In any case, that Expulsion had caused so much trudging along strange ways; how long had it taken until a few souls of some later generation had found their way to Singapore? And now she had left that place behind, too.

But the year 1492 had other, more relevant significance. Safed was said to have been a sleepy, inactive nothingness. However, in that year, perhaps by sheer coincidence, perhaps due to tidings of the Expulsion – she didn't know – the little town was reorganized. Great rabbis began to flock there in the wake of the scholarly work that was gaining momentum and, with it, fame.

It was in that same year, 1492, that the Christian theologian, Erasmus of Rotterdam, was ordained priest in his monastery. But Erasmus died in 1536, the year which saw the dissolution of the monasteries in England. And then 1536 was the year when Joseph Caro settled in Safed; he was author of the *Shulhan Aruch*, the great work that codified Jewish law for all future generations.

And, perhaps most important of Safed's rabbis, was Isaac Lurie, the Kabbalist who settled in the place in 1570. He taught the importance of profound mental concentration during the performance of religious duties; only thus, he felt, could real links with the God of Israel be forged and the Jewish rites truly sanctified.

"Cruelty, greed and callousness in Spain and Europe," said Esther to herself, "and spiritual intellectuality here in tiny Safed."

(Where now was Ora's father, that poor, incoherent old peddler with his claim to connection with famous rabbis? How he would have delighted to take part in such discourse!)

Mrs. Kordovi did not consider herself a learned woman; she would laugh at herself as a "scholar of bits and pieces" – but it was just such bits and pieces of Jewish thought that had bound the dispersed nation wherever they were; and she found these ironies and coincidences of history fascinating, in any case.

However, she had not come to live in the past, recall it as she might. She had come to join her people in building a new future.

Stationed on a hilltop within sight of the small flat she had rented, on the outskirts of the little town, was a platoon of British soldiers (Palestine was still under the Mandatory Power), and some Jewish lads among them. Here was a satisfactory task for her: On weekdays she would invite a few young men to tea, English style, as she had known it in Singapore, and she would have the Jewish soldiers over for a proper Friday night or Festival Eve. They could make *Kiddush*, say Grace after the meal. Jew and Gentile, so far from home, would get this slight touch of home. At least as long as the war lasted, her life would have some meaning. Later, something else would surely present itself. Esther was pleased with her decision to make her home in Safed.

On summer evenings the air would turn cool, and she often needed to wear a sweater. Nor had she known how cold it could get in winter, especially in contrast to the climate of hot Singapore. Also, there was no real twilight here in this Holy Land; this was quite unlike the gradually fading late afternoons of other countries. She was glad of that, for twilight can be a sentimentally hurtful hour to the lonely. But long evenings need to be filled with something more than the egotistical enjoyment of reading.

She would knit. These young lads who enjoyed her teatime during the week, or her Friday night festive dinner, they could do with some warmer clothes: socks or an undervest, or something of the sort. Esther set out shopping one morning. Along the main street of the city there was a row of small shops, but none of them stocked wool or knitting needles.

"I'll ask at the grocer's, he will surely be able to direct me." The grocer knew this tall, loose-limbed lady who came in for bread, milk and other such modest items. She always entered with a smile, was so gracious in her way of addressing him, so considerate in paying on the spot, never asking for anything "to be charged till next month"; such customers were a pleasure to deal with, a real aristocratic lady she was. Unusual.

Her request now was also unusual: Where could she get wool and knitting needles? Could he just show her the way, if it wasn't too much bother?

It was her turn to be surprised:

"You can get them here," said the grocer, opening a small cupboard. Knitting needles in a grocery store? This would be a small, funny item of news the next time she wrote to her daughter.

Meanwhile, the vendor had set out a few pairs of knitting needles of various sizes, as well as some skeins of knitting wool. She picked out what suited her, but looked up rather shocked when told the price.

"That's expensive," Esther remarked, comparing the sum with what she used to pay in Singapore.

The man swept the items off the counter and turned to her as if insulted. He had not expected that comment from this gracious lady.

"If you will find them at a cheaper rate anywhere else," he exclaimed, "come back to me and I shall let you have them gratis."

Esther bought them, of course. This would certainly fill an interesting letter! Fancy finding such things in a grocery store – and getting such a response. The grocer, counting out the change and wrapping up the goods in an old newspaper (looking it over first to make sure he had read it), noticed a puzzling expression as he handed the package to his customer; was it amusement or annoyance? But why should she laugh at him? And what was there to annoy her? She could certainly afford it, and, after all, he had to make a living.

"Funny people, these newcomers from Heaven knows where," was his silent comment as she bid him "Shalom."

Funny, this particular newcomer? Could they have sat down together (with that old London peddler), they might soon have become embroiled in a knowledgeable discussion on the work of the famous "Arie," Rabbi Isaac Lurie. But neither grocer nor peddler could have picked out Singapore on the map; the forebears of both grocer and Londoner had come from some small place in the Russian Pale of Settlement where geography had not been a subject for study in the *Heder*.

And the grocer's grandparents had come to study with the eminent rabbis whose work made the little Safed become known as one of the four Holy Cities of the ancient homeland.

* *
*

Vered in a scene of toil and moil

Once Vered had loved the sunshine. To her child's eyes it had revealed glorious color. That had changed now. The sun was to be avoided, shunned as if it were as outcast as the Jews of Europe. It was hot at noon in the sandy settlement, and the workmen had been laboring since before dawn.

"Heat must drive out heat," declared Vered as, in the heat of the day, she poured great tumblers of steaming lemon tea. Then, noticing the skeptical, not to say surly glances of the laborers as they eyed the rising steam, she would add in a tone of persuasion:

"That's what My Old Lady always said."

But what had her Old Lady known of physical toil under a relentless sun? An ice-cold drink was what they wanted. They could hardly hold the hot glasses in their hands. Being thirsty, they drank till soon the sweat dampened their skin – and, after all, there was something refreshing in it. She was a good woman, this Vered, they would say no rough words in her presence; but at home, in the evenings, they would ask their wives in scorn:

"Did her Old Lady think this wasteland was a ladies' drawing-room where one balanced the cup delicately on a napkin-covered knee?"

The men were too occupied sucking the lumps of ice that fell on their tongues as they swallowed the popular mead of the time to notice their wives smiling. In that period most of the group had, indeed, come from German towns where families had had "Ladies' Drawing Rooms."

Her "Old Lady"! The idea that the Old Lady had known nothing of that far place called Palestine, had not found it necessary to imbue her granddaughter with Jewish knowledge or Zionist ideals, never entered their minds. Nor Vered's either. She had seen how her husband looked when he had told her to pack, and she had been like an automaton ever since, aware of little more than that life had become harsh, but her children were safe.

Mentally adrift in this strange, different kind of life in an unfamiliar environment, Vered kept strictly to the wisdom imparted by her Old Lady during a childhood when all she had wanted was the courage to rebel openly. Today, however, these old-fashioned maxims helped her steer her way through this – to her – alien world. Should she move blindly through time, from task to task, like a robot? Let them mock her if it gave them pleasure.

So, if their singlets clung damp to their chests and the perspiration dripped from their foreheads, here was good, hot tea. Heat must drive out heat!

"But things are not the same here," the hardiest would exclaim, "it wasn't so hot where you come from."

And primly, Vered would quote:

"Accusing the circumstances is but excusing one's self."

"Oh, she's talking philosophy," said those early pioneers, and returned to their tasks, murmuring, none too quietly, that one could hardly expect a member of the "Saloon Society" to understand the need for change.

Happening once to be visiting there, Fräulein laughed.

"Unless you mean the workers who frequent the pubs of England," she told them, "and get drunk so often, I don't know what you mean by 'Saloon Society.' There is no such thing."

She had not been in the country long enough to make allowances for nuances of pronunciation. Like Malka, who laughed at herself for imagining that *"Lo yodéa"* meant "Not Jewish," so Fräulein later took herself to task for not recognizing "Saloon" as being meant for "Salon." The hefty laborers, struggling with the roots of prickly thistles to clear a ditch for the laying down of pipes, said among themselves:

"Naive young girl! What does she know of life? She thinks it so romantic."

In fact, she found it rather funny. She would write to her family over the sea that "there is a country of Jews here, but it isn't really a Jewish country. The people are all different, they just don't understand one another."

"Appearances are deceptive," came the reply from a thousand miles away, "of course Jews are building a Jewish country!" Well!

Vered loved little children and would, when she managed it, hand out little packets of sweets.

"But you can't afford it," a neighbor would gently admonish, "and the child gets enough at home."

"But a child has such a small fist," Vered would reply earnestly. "It's so easily filled. My Old Lady taught me that."

Did she make confiture from fruit that had not been sold? Her Old Lady had taught her that, too, that everything can be put to some purpose. Various articles had to be purchased? And most likely the money in hand would not suffice? Here, too, her Old Lady, so long dead, buried so far away, again came to the rescue:

"Sometimes," she had taught her granddaughter, "money is money – but sometimes money is rubbish. One must know how to distinguish."

Vered learned to distinguish. Her little daughter needed a blouse for Shabbat and certain school ceremonies? Vered possessed one embroidered nightgown stacked away; it had been one of many in Berlin, but who needed it here in the sand? Out of a lingering sentimentality she had packed it in at the last moment. Now the nightie could be cut up and made into a blouse for the little one. Money was freed for some other purpose.

But Vered would not count money when her husband became ill and had to be hospitalized in Tel Aviv, half an hour's bus ride away. She would not leave her little ones at home while she sat by their father's bedside; cost what it might, they would stay with her in the big city. Seeing them around his bed might give him the courage to bear his pain and conquer the illness.

The money was spent – and the three came back alone to the house on the sands after the funeral.

She now had to wake up, the time for carrying out her daily chores automaton-like was over. Again she recalled her Old Lady declaring:

"When the father dies, the breadwinner goes. But when the mother dies, the children are left with nothing!"

There was no comfort for her in the words; bitter experience had taught Vered their truth. Her children must not be allowed to remain with nothing. But how could she ensure that?

This account, so far, is ordinary, maybe even banal. Such tragedies have happened to women the world over. Vered's isn't even so very different from the fate of Esther Kordovi, except that the latter did not need to worry about her offspring.

Banal? But you were special, Vered, so very special.

* * *

Malka listens to a tale of eating

It was the nature of our Majestic Malka to mother every young person who came within her orbit. Now, with her daughter married and her son Heaven knew where, she attached herself to the young girl she knew only as Fräulein, and who seemed so alone. A Jewish girl from England, that was rather unusual in those days. Stranger still, the girl already spoke Hebrew, she even spoke German, though with an English accent that gave it a strange attraction. While bathing her heat blisters, Malka asked questions: How had a girl so young come to leave her family? Did her parents not object? Had she no relatives out here?

Oh, she had been offered a job and she liked the notion of travelling, and certainly of being so independent. No, her parents had not objected, they were devoted Zionists. And yes, she knew someone living in one of the new little settlements not so far from Tel Aviv.

Three sentences. Not a very open person, thought Malka, she's Jewish, but so English in her ways. Always reserved, these English.

But then the girl began to laugh:

"I must tell you about my last Shabbat. Just imagine, I had to eat three full dinners, one after another!"

Her parents had sent her to bid farewell to an aunt in the neighborhood and then to her grandmother just up the way. She was instructed to be back for the family dinner by around one o'clock.

It had been a day of clear sunshine, one of those rare summer days in London. Mid-morning, that last Saturday, she walked across the park. It wasn't much of a park, really, just a broad area of well-kept grass on one side of the pathway and tennis courts on the other. But there were benches along the way, so that the old folk could sit and gossip and feel something of a country atmosphere, rare for that district.

Her aunt insisted that she join the family there for the *Shabbes* meal. It was useless to refuse – she would be travelling the next day, and it might be years before she saw them again. She was placed at the head of the table, the guest of honor for the first time in her life. Her uncle and cousins plied her with questions, while her aunt piled her plate with food.

"What was she going to do out there?"

"Didn't she know that Arab rioting was going on?"

"What were her parents thinking of to let her go at such a time?"

She felt so important. And with her ship's ticket and her visa as tangible items in her purse, the Arab rioting in the Holy Land in that year of 1936 was no more than newsprint to her.

She could not linger, she still had to get to her grandmother. Kisses all around, tears in the eyes of her aunt, good wishes in chorus – and then back across the park. She should have known the old lady would not let her go so easily:

"What! Your last *Shabbes* and you will not eat with me?"

Grandma was a lonely widow; how could she be refused? It was almost twelve-thirty, and she had to be home in forty minutes at the latest – and she had already eaten at her aunt's.

"There yes, and with me no?" Grandma made valiant efforts to speak English – and this logic was unassailable! So, once more there was the hot golden broth to be swallowed, the browned chicken leg swimming in fat – who had ever thought of cholesterol then? – the crisp baked potatoes, the honey-sweetened carrots.

Again kisses, tears, blessings, and heavy sighs: Would she ever see this grandchild, her first, again? Being a wise woman, she had an inkling that this departure was likely to be the start of a process that would split the close-knit family; on the other hand, perhaps it was for the best that the girl was on her way to the land of her own people – was there not an Evil One threatening from just across the sea, and an Oswald Mosley right here? The Master of the Universe would protect this young girl from the evil that was on its way.

It was only a short walk down the road to home. They would not scold the girl for being late on this, her last day. But the consumption of two full meals within the last couple of hours was no excuse for not partaking of the festive meal her mother had specially prepared.

Telling Malka about it now, she could not help but laugh. Fancy eating three heavy meals, one after another; it was funny. But the very heaviness in her stomach had, at the time, enhanced her unwonted feeling of being "someone." She knew the comment on her unobtrusive manners: "This girl always enters unnoticed, she sits here so quietly, and no one notices that she has gone out, that she is not here in the room anymore."

She knew that the mockery was affectionate. She had been brought up to such conduct. It belonged to the period – or rather, as she later thought, to her parents' period.

"*Na, ja,*" was Malka's only comment, but to herself she thought:

"So they are afraid of Nazism even in England! Her family was right to let the girl go when the chance offered itself."

Malka was too aware of her own reluctance to let her daughter join the Maccabi group, yet now she wished her son had joined, too. Except that this English Fräulein had brought along across the sea a huge boxful of books, she never found out much more about her.

* * *

Ora in a scene of her own

Ora could never stand fireworks. She found no fun and saw no beauty in the sparkling shower of color that lit up a stretch of the sky before vanishing earthward into nothingness. She would remain indoors with the curtains closed whenever a celebration promised – or, as she considered it, threatened a show of fireworks. They recalled too vividly the bombing of London, after two years of which she had enlisted in the Land Army.

A town girl, Ora was sent for a time to learn what farming and land work were all about. There was satisfaction in planting vegetable seeds and seeing the green little shoots peeping out of the earth later, but the soil had to be properly prepared beforehand, and town girls in general did not favor the smell of manure. Beautiful stretches of smoothly mown grass needed to be uprooted for the sowing, if the people of Britain were to be adequately fed when shipping could not be spared for importing produce. There is delight in picking fresh fruit from trees, but the trees have to be pruned, sprayed and cared for with the necessary nutrients.

Ora had to learn all this and more. Farming meant feeding chickens and cleaning out their coops, not merely collecting eggs.

It also required dealing with pigs, with cows and yes – with feminine jealousy!

See now this Jewish girl: She is sturdily built, nicely proportioned in shape, has dark, curly hair and dark, dreamy eyes. She is the daughter of an alien Jew steeped in Jewish knowledge, understanding Talmud and the laws of *Shmitta* – the seventh year, when land should lie fallow – and curiously interested in Kabbalist mysticism.

Note how she takes the piglets her father would have shuddered at, one under each arm, and carries them across to the sty where they will be cared for – until their turn comes to be sent to market. She learns to milk cows and finds this satisfying. Her fingers are strong, the cows respond, and babies in the British Isles will get their rations. She gains confidence in her ability to do this work, it suits her absolutely.

What she is uncertain of is the attitude of the farmer's wife. She senses hostility but ignores what she fails to comprehend. Ora likes milking cows. She is scrupulous in measuring quantities and reckoning the cost of each pasteurized pint. Her strict honesty in collecting the milk money evoked the farmer's warm praise; he had been cheated often enough. But once, while she was sterilizing the bottles, her hair got caught in the machine and she yelled for help.

Later, as if in jest, the farmer's wife remarked: "Your hair got caught? My, I thought you were singing. Your voice is that strong."

Her head still hurting, Ora stared at her in surprise. Only now did she notice that the woman was heavy with child and was looking with undisguised envy at Ora's flat stomach. This display of jealousy amused Ora; she had scarcely an idea of what the farmer looked like, all her attention had been paid to the cattle she was learning to care for.

Hidden in the wooded countryside in the vicinity of that farming area, there was an internment camp for German prisoners of war. Sometimes working nearby, Ora would notice some of the internees and, not thinking of their nationality at all, felt how hard it had to be to have one's freedom so restricted. She hated restriction, never able to forget the tiny flat in which she had been cooped up with her sister in London, or the shabby old house crowded with family.

The broad, green stretch of open country was heaven to her, she knew she would never again want to live inside four cramping walls.

Perhaps that was why, subconsciously, she could not find her way to the tiny room she rented in Jerusalem some years later.

Just now, she was gratefully aware of her freedom from town life – and could not help wondering how these mostly young prisoners could bear to be deprived of the liberty to run through the woods, or race along the country lanes, or buy postcards, stamps and cigarettes at the village store.

Ora was an intensely emotional being, too young and immature for objective thinking. When she saw a young man gazing at the world outside his fenced-in area, she saw nothing more than the yearning in his eyes. She dared then, giving scarcely a thought to any supervisor who might be hovering, to go across and give the prisoner some small delicacy she had saved from her own rations. Land Army girls were allotted slightly better menus than townsfolk – and certainly better ones than the POWs. Noting how gratefully these little extras were received, she continued the practice whenever she could. Helping was her basic human instinct.

But – there is so often a "but" in even the simplest of human matters.

"You look Jewish," declared one such prisoner to whom she was handing a small packet.

"Of course I'm Jewish," she confirmed.

He threw the packet in her face, muttering some imprecations not loud enough for the words to carry across the air, yet no less understandable. Thereafter, whenever he noticed her working in the field near the camp grounds, he turned away too pointedly for

Ora to ignore the inimical action. And yet – he did not know her at all, no more than she knew him.

Then she wondered: Had that farmer's wife known Ora was Jewish and disliked her simply for that? Or had the woman really been jealous on hearing her husband praise the flat-bellied young girl?

Unlike the incoherent father whom Ora hardly knew, at least not in the way girls generally know their fathers, she had little knowledge of her national tradition and culture, nor indeed much interest in it.

It took two hostile strangers to rouse her to the Jewishness that meant so little to her.

Ora did a lot of thinking. The war would be coming to its end, that could not be far off now. Her mother had died a year earlier, her sister was thinking of marriage and would care for their father. Her brothers had gone their various ways.

Horrid pictures of German atrocities were beginning to appear in newspapers and on the newsreels of cinema screens. Ora would soon be virtually on her own.

She knew what she would do when this ugly war ended: She would volunteer for social work in mentally diseased, psychic Europe; her energy would go where it was needed – to the survivors of those unimaginable camps.

* *
*

Malka in a scene of problem

Work, hard work and lots of it – that is one sure way of getting through innumerable days when the heart aches with worry that is both definite and yet uncertain. In the distance, one doesn't know just where, beloved ones are trapped by the Evil Ones. But where? And what kind of evil? The rumors that whisper of dread are impossible to believe.

"No. Such things just can't happen."

Our Majestic Malka found herself a new job, one that would give her less leisure. She would be housekeeper to a private family. Planning and cooking meals, ordering the ingredients, catering festive, formal dinners and late-night receptions – all this would keep her busy enough to fall into bed at night with aching feet and eyes that closed even while she was undressing.

Best of all, she was allowed no more than one half-day off weekly. Then she could visit her family or go with Fräulein to the Armon cinema in Haifa. It had a movable roof that would be rolled back in hot weather, so that for the price of one's ticket one could often see the starry sky above as well as the film. In those days films all came from abroad and were dubbed with the Hebrew translation; if one could only exercise greater powers of concentration, one could pick up some Hebrew, too, for the same ticket.

Then there was the fifteen-minute interval in the middle of the film. Thronging around the "buffet" in the entrance hall for coffee or ice cream added to the pleasure of that half-day off. It was a far cry from the ornately carpeted floors, the plush seats and ornamented galleries of Viennese or London cinemas, even from the "flicks" of the poorer London districts. Here, in Haifa's cinemas, heels tapped noisily on the hard, tiled floors, but the seed-spitting brought in by the flood of post-war immigrants had not yet become endemic. Going to a film or sitting in a café were about all one could do on that precious "half-day off."

Malka took special enjoyment in both of these "amusements," because they enabled her to observe the population. Nearly everyone was young. Seldom did one see elderly folk about, and Malka looked at these youthful Jews with a motherly eye. Her heart ached for the teenaged girls dressed so simply in the cotton button-ups stitched in the small bayside factory. She admired the sturdy young men who worked so hard and lived so frugally: a small jar of curds and a heaped plateful of mashed potatoes satisfied them. Coffee and cake in a café was all the relaxation they seemed to require. Few people appeared to have families, and along one Haifa street there were more restaurants than shops, the tables always full of chattering youngsters uncomplainingly enjoying their simple fare.

Meanwhile, every lonesome young person who got to know this majestic-looking lady soon perceived that here was a woman one could turn to for help or advice.

There was Rivka, for instance, who, for a small wage, carried heavy bags of groceries from the cluttered grocery store to the customers' houses.

In every kitchen she would be offered a cold drink before the housewife let her take up the heavy bag again and continue her deliveries. Who had a car in those days? But Rivka, recently married, often left Malka's package, heavy as it was, till the end of her round, knowing that here she could unload a different kind of burden. Once she wanted a recipe for a meal "that would hardly cost anything," and once she wanted advice on making an old skirt look more presentable. This time her problem was more serious: "My husband is out many evenings, playing cards with his friends," she told Malka rather bashfully. "I know I can't expect him not to see his pals just because he got married. But this carrying makes me so tired, and then, when I've done the housework, I have to spend many evenings alone. The empty flat makes me irritable…"

Malka spared her the embarrassment of completing the sentence. Rivka had jutting teeth and a receding chin. There was a dearth of women in the land at that time, girls had no trouble finding a mate.

Malka found it important that Rivka's husband should be glad to have a wife and a home.

"Listen to me," she commanded, "tell your man to bring his friends home once or twice a week. Bake a cake. Sit apart from the men with some sewing or knitting. So you will be resting. But keep your ears open, you have to know what they are talking about, what interests them. After some time, say an hour or so, bring in the cake and coffee. Then sit down, talk to the men, cut cake for yourself, too, and drink your coffee with them. Then clear the table, go back to your needlework and let them get on with their cards. You will see how proud your husband will be. The married men will expect the same of their wives, and soon you will have a whole circle of friends. You'll even be glad of an evening to yourself now and then."

"How wise this woman is," thought Rivka as she kissed her, checked the groceries and went her way.

Malka soon became a welcome visitor in many such small homes.

On one occasion, however, her wisdom failed her. Fräulein, happening to be in the neighborhood, thought she'd drop in for a brief visit. But as she approached the kitchen door, she heard a loud altercation and hesitated to enter. Malka's deep voice was heard protesting:

"But, Sir, I do *not* belong to any union."

To which the master's stentorian tones declared in what he intended to be German – but was merely his notion that to speak German one had simply to change the sound of the vowels and consonants:

"Ick smoll oonyen!"

And Malka, not so majestic now, reiterated somewhat pathetically:

"Sir, believe me, I have nothing to do with any union."

"Oonyen" to Malka had only one meaning. The master was becoming angry:

"Ick smoll oonyen. Ick no vill oonyen!"

To herself, Malka was thinking: "I wish I did belong to a union, you'd have to pay me better wages."

But the master read something else in her expression, something like defiance. He did not intend to let her refute the charge and exploded in the English she had never learned:

"How dare you say there are no onions when I smell them?"

He stormed out of the kitchen, not noticing the Fräulein giggling nearby. For her to have entered the kitchen and intervened would have been an unheard-of impertinence. She now went in and explained to the unhappy housekeeper, who feared for her job, that the master simply objected to the smell of onions – they happened to be sizzling aromatically in the pan as he had passed the kitchen.

Good cooking without onions? What would the meat taste like? There was a problem for our Majestic Malka to work out!

* * *

Girl in trouble of her own

Nor could the learned Fräulein help her here. Onions had been a normal part of cooking ingredients. She had, indeed, brought over a boxful of her favorite books, as well as dictionaries and reference books – but nary a cookbook among them. One of her reference books, she thought, might be useful in explaining why onions did smell so strongly and made one's eyes water (if not the master's mouth).

And now she learned something: She was amazed to discover that both words – onion and union – originated in the same Latin root *unus*, meaning "one": An onion is one sphere, it has no core, and no matter how many layers one peels off, one goes on peeling until no layers of skin remain. This information made the incident all the funnier, especially when she learnt that scallions were – local food! Onions from Askelon.

Well, this knowledge would help neither maid nor master, it was no more than Fräulein being Fräulein. Besides, she had a small problem of her own just then. She had become acquainted with some young folk of her own age with whom she sometimes spent one of her own rare half-days off.

To her surprise, she found herself something of a sensation to them. They simply could not believe that a Jew born in England where, by all accounts, Jews were not molested and were free to practice Judaism, and could even rise to important posts without needing to be baptized, that such a one would leave that developed country for this harsh little patch of sand, rock, thorns and thistles, from which problems in diverse abundance sprouted regularly. Not only this, but the young lady had announced her intention of staying.

One of the group decided that this unusual person just had to be seen by his mother, to whom "English" meant the not always so friendly clerks of the Mandatory Authority.

Malka urged the girl to accept the invitation; perhaps the youth's East European mother knew something about onionless cookery? Would Fräulein ask her? There must be some way of making a dainty dish fit for her Gentile master!

But on this weighty topic the lad's mother proved unapproachable. She had inquiries of her own to make. Her son had been talking too much in praise of this English girl, so strangely known as Fräulein – which was no name at all, and certainly suitable neither for the period nor the place. Still, she would welcome her son's friend, it was incumbent on Jews to be hospitable, was it not? So as soon as the young lady arrived and had been greeted, the inevitable glass of tea – wet, light brownish and sweet – was set before her.

The guest had been in Haifa long enough to be ready for what, in her mind, she termed "Sabra water"; she was polite enough to sip it, slowly, a tiny sip at a time, not letting her distaste show on her face. But then the questions began and the gaps between sips grew longer; her hostess was subjecting her, she felt, to a kind of catechism:

"Where do you live?

"On the Carmel? That's nice. Is it your own flat?

"Ah, you just rent it. How many rooms are there?

"Are they big rooms? Do you share with anyone?

"No? You live alone? Are your rooms nicely furnished?

"Did you bring the furniture from England?

"Is it expensive? Is the rent high?

"How much do you pay?"

At this point, the older woman should have noticed the girl frowning as she put down her half-full glass. But the next query took its expected course:

"Do you get good wages?

"How much do you earn?"

No, this was too much. Her face innocent of guile, Fräulein volunteered some information of her own:

"You know, my father takes size ten in socks but size eleven in shoes. Isn't that funny?"

Her interlocutor now took a good hard look at her son's friend. The girl's face showed only a sweet complaisance.

"Why do you tell me that?" asked the mother sharply.

"I thought you wanted to know. You've been asking me so many details."

Mother got up from her seat with dignity and walked to the door. As she passed her son's chair, she commented none too softly:

"*Meshuggene Engländerin!* (Crazy Englishwoman!)"

And, naturally, Fräulein also got up to leave. She would treasure this memory of how a friendship came to its end. But the young man needed to defend his mother; he also had a reasonable explanation:

"You should know, here we Jews are like one family. We are always interested in one another, especially in newcomers. It's not like over there, where nobody cares a damn about us."

Maybe. Maybe there was something in that. Just the same, they would not meet again.

And nonetheless, that last sentence of his came back to her with force not so many years later. She was reading the daily English newspaper and found a small paragraph, almost hidden among the newsprint crowded around it. The paper bore the date, Thursday, February 13th, 1945, and here is the paragraph:

> "*Truckloads of children were burnt alive by the Germans at Auschwitz (Oswiecim) concentration*

camp, 30 miles east of Cracow, and mothers who witnessed the spectacle went mad..."

Malka, dear Majestic Malka, may you never see this paragraph, may it not appear in your German news-sheet; may you never learn a word of English; never ask anyone to translate parts of the English paper for you. You had a little grandson and a daughter-in-law.

* * *

Vered, too, must learn to cope

Throughout that week of mourning for husband and father, neighbors came in and out all the day and every day, leaving food in the kitchen, murmuring kind words. Vered, as was only to be expected, sat on her low stool, stunned, bewildered, seldom uttering a word. Young as they were, the two children wondered at their mother; it was the first time that they felt as if she were far from them, in some unknown place, unaware of their presence.

They had never seen her so, and Fräulein, who noticed everything, took them both back with her to Haifa, so that they should feel cared for, until Vered came to grips with life again. And, naturally, when she awoke to the realization that she was alone in her house, no one was sleeping in any of the beds, she knew she had to develop some sense of purpose. A totally empty house was not to be borne.

For a small share of the returns, a neighbor offered to look after her orange grove which adjoined his own. Fruit trees, as well as rows of vegetables, had been planted around the house for the family's use; now, after all the years of tireless tending, Vered could dispense with the greater part of her produce, selling it to shops and markets. Hopefully, they would manage. She might even get a day's work now and then in the clinic or babysitting.

But she needed to hear the voices of her children. She had to bring them home.

The skies were cloudy as she boarded the bus for Haifa; it was an early winter day, and as she came into the town, the rain began to fall. Vered, for the first time in her life, looked at the rain with something like gladness. To her children's surprise, she declared:

"It isn't rain. It is liquid gold sent down from Heaven to help us. If it keeps on for a few days, we won't need to irrigate or water our plot. That's a great saving."

Thereafter, rain was always "liquid gold" in the small family. Vered no longer looked up to admire the blue of the summer sky, nor did the allure of a blue silk dress ever again form a picture in her mind. As news of the war in Europe was bringing more than mere anxiety or disquiet to Jews wherever they lived, Vered became grateful for the peacefulness of the village that had been built in that stretch of sand. There were many houses now, each with its plot of vegetables, melons, trees and, here and there, a daring housewife had even planted a few flowers. She could look around, remember and take pride in what had been achieved.

If only she could have let her husband know how grateful she was for his foresight in taking them out of Germany so soon. This time it was not her Old Lady but Vered's own, heartfelt sincerity that uttered advice to every young lass she knew:

"When you marry, remember to praise your husband for everything good, no matter how trivial it may be. Because once he closes his eyes, there is no more to be said. You are left contrite, and there is nothing you can do about it."

Vered never tried to learn Hebrew, she just couldn't put her mind to it; but as most of the villagers had come from Germany, she had no problem communicating. A hint of a sparkle in those once impish eyes would give way to a quiet pride, as she admitted (as so many did then) that "it was easier to feel ashamed of her inability to speak Hebrew than to learn it, but both children speak it beautifully, and they are bilingual as well!"

"Both children." This was her greatest worry. How could she, without her cultured husband, without a breadwinner, give them that standard of education that she owed them? The thought that they would have less learning than their parents was unacceptable.

To add to her worries, the growing ferocity of the war now demanded for itself the shipping which had exported the ever-popular "Jaffas." Her grove brought in a smaller income that continually ate up what had to be invested in it. Without export, the grove soaked up the "liquid gold" in winter and the cost of irrigation during the rest of the year. This little Middle East country has a short winter, and the rest of the year it is dry. Disposal of the fruit became a problem; selling it cheaply on the market or to jam factories hardly paid her way. Certainly it did not compensate her for the outlay or the work.

Still, as is their habit, the years passed, and even that war, with its horrors, its unbelievable sadism, its incredible cruelty, the strangely callous, uncaring response to the cruelty – even that war came to its end, leaving its horrific aftermath.

* *
*

Interlude

While letting our players rest awhile, it is only fair to utter a warning. This is not a narrative with a plot. The lives of our characters may or may not intertwine. What binds them is their membership of the one extended family that is the Jewish nation.

Furthermore, they are unlikely to do anything that is considered heroic in these days. They will not spend energy on kicking a ball around; they will not punch anyone's bulging muscles; they will not even, half-clad, tear one another's hair out on the perilous edge of a bathing pool. To no one's prurient curiosity will they reveal how they show passion for any men. Lesbianism will have no place in this account – and, probably, there are other symbols of our modern "culture" of which readers will be deprived.

What, then, is the point here? Well, to be honest, it derives – the whole story – from a picture.

Somewhere in one of Europe's cold, northern countries, a person must have screamed. Screamed terribly. And a painter in Norway, named Munch, painted that scream. Painted it so graphically that, marvelling, one looks at the silent canvas and one actually hears the horrific scream! Was it a human being in agony? Or was it his own perception of the human race in anguish that set the artist's tactile senses tingling?

Whatever it was, the painter (we can only imagine) rushed to his studio to depict the visage of a living soul in unbearable despair. He painted a face in the throes of such suffering as an onlooker can hardly grasp.

Here another "small crumb of cogitation" cries out for articulation: We are told that civilization in Scandinavia developed later than elsewhere, on account of the denser ice there melting more slowly than in the more southern parts of our world. But when human life did appear in that cold north, it made quick advance. The archeologists who researched the Stone Age up there discovered not only the expected remnants of food, but other signs of human progress: They found weapons.

Even at that early stage, the clues to civilization were not different from those of today: fear, attack and defense.

And development has been steady. Measured by the pace of history, which has its own time measurement, the progress has come in leaps and bounds. Research of the Stone Age in that cold north revealed burial pits in which numbers of corpses lie together. Already then, communal inhumation disposed of the dead. But did all those lying in one pit die at the same time?

It is but a leap, measured, as said, by the pace of history, and passing over the human remains of the multitudes killed in wars at all stages of time, to the mass graves of the Nazi war. Numberless bodies, dead or with a gasp of breath still in them, were pitched or shot by human beasts into huge pits. Defenseless Jews had been forced, brutally, to dig these graves for their own selves. Did they scream? Did anyone hear?

And from these mass graves, it is but a very short jump (again, measured by history's own pace), just a hop-scotch sort of jump, to the dismembered limbs, the odd head suddenly blown off its shoulders, the severed arm or foot, the bits and pieces of human flesh, the blood spattered over soil and paving.

Did such heroic deeds leave an instant of time for screaming? They were carried out in our own days, here in our own homeland, by wicked young fools persuaded by their priestly imams that such murderous acts of "glory" would bring them straight to paradise. The young fools were also led to believe that some scores of virgins were there awaiting the "manliness" of these "martyred" suicide bombers. By the way, where did these virgins come from?

Knowledge of these things set us wondering. That portrait by Munch has been and remains the backdrop to all the scenes depicted in this narrative. What was in the painter's mind when his hand traced so terrible a scream on his silent canvas? Was he prophesying, or was he criticizing past history? Humankind cannot really be very proud of its war-marked past. As for the present, it doesn't bear thinking of with any degree of equanimity. Killing and murder introduced this twentieth century, and there seems no end to the criminality of it all.

Life itself has become no more sacred than it ever was. The means of killing become ever more sophisticated. Men build and men destroy – and do not give a thought to the foolishness of it.

Yes, technology today eases so many of our former work loads. We have merely to learn which knobs or buttons to press – and behold! The work is done, the garments clean, the food cooked, figures in ledgers are totted up, multiplied and divided at the touch of a finger; and even communication with those living thousands of miles away is achieved in minutes – brief and emotionless though it be.

And with it all, no one has any time. Folk are always "too busy," they rush around like hordes of hyper-actives. The latchkey children eat junk food and fast food, and there is much talk of vitamins, of cholesterol and the like. Becoming or remaining "slim and slender" has turned into an earnest aim of life – even while drink and drug addiction do and will do far greater damage to mind and physique.

Who can tell to what kind of future all this leads? Will screaming help? Who screams? And for what reason?

So let us return to our simple friends, the once impish Vered, the aristocratic Esther, our majestic Viennese Malka and the idealistic Ora.

Then there is the strange, ubiquitous Fräulein who does nothing, but tries to understand things.

Hush now, the curtain goes up again; there is a figure on the stage.

* *
*

Backdrop – Picture of a Scream by Munch

Esther in a scene of basic energy

The hateful war had ended in Europe. As Esther Kordovi had known, the platoon of British soldiers was to be moved from that naked hilltop. The Mandatory Authorities were probably making their own plans for the future of Palestine, and unrest among the Arabs was in the air; they were planning to take Safed for themselves. Who dreamt that the few Jews in the country could stand up and defend their home with a purposeful spirit that would defy every effort to stop them?

Before long, Esther hoped, she would be able to buy her plot of land up on the little hill and build the house she had dreamt of.

Since the purchase of knitting needles in the grocery store, Esther had written a great many letters to her family in England. She liked them to have a picture of the various types of Jews she met in synagogue, in shops, in the narrow alleys of Safed. And she always tried to include an amusing anecdote to ensure that her letters were lively. The small place was a veritable gossip-land where everyone knew what everyone was doing, thinking, even dreaming.

The latest joke making the rounds was of the poor worker who dreamt one night that with the coming of peace he would construct a huge factory and employ lots of workers. He woke up to the reality of his bread, margarine and curds for breakfast, the dream fading completely from his memory as he turned on his wireless set to listen to the news of the day. Then he went to his dull job.

As he entered the shabby old workshop, a fellow worker hailed him with the greeting:

"Shalom, Dovidl! When will you be opening your factory? Would you let me buy a share? How much would I need to invest?"

Poor Dovidl scarcely knew what the man was talking about.

Esther never delayed sending off a letter once it was written, so she went to the Post Office where she bought a few more of the open sheets on which letters were written in wartime. The authorities made miniature photocopies of these, so that the weight of the entire mail was greatly reduced for wartime despatch; the letters were enlarged to normal size before distribution. This practice ended when shipping and plane service returned to normal, but it had given birth to the cheap and useful aerogram.

On her way, Esther bought her copy of the daily newspaper to read leisurely with her mid-morning coffee.

But her coffee was left to grow cold as she stared unbelievingly at the headline in bold black print: A bomb had been dropped on "an important army base in Japan, a bomb which represented the basic energy of the universe."

She read those words again: the basic energy of the universe. That is what it took to force Japan's surrender? To stop the killing, the satanic sadism that tormented and tortured powerless little humans? How bad can men be? It was hard to comprehend. But what did it mean, "the basic energy of the universe"? Such a bomb surely caused terrible suffering to people who had had no say in any war-making decisions.

She thought of her Benedict, gone to his rest before the iniquity overtook mankind. If his grave in Singapore had not been desecrated, he was resting where for some years the forces of evil had held sway. She imagined herself asking him in formidable seriousness:

"What is this basic energy of the universe? Why is it used for the destruction of life?"

And she knew what his reply would have been: "Women don't understand these things."

Esther smiled as she "heard" the familiar words. But with the smiling, she felt a resentment rise. Why should women even try to understand these things? Women brought forth life. How were they supposed to understand its destruction? Its wilful destruction.

Then she drew out of a file the newspaper of December 16th, 1945, which she had purposely kept. It told of the murder of six million Jews in Europe. The German Major Wilhelm Hoettl had attested to this in his affidavit to the War Crimes Tribunal. In his evidence he had declared that Himmler had been dissatisfied, the animal had hoped the number would be greater.

Esther asked herself why "the basic energy of the universe" had not been employed to put a stop to Nazi brutality before it reached this stage of savagery.

Well, did she want it used or not? Just a moment earlier she had been shocked. She was at odds with herself, she realized. She had seen the anguish, the deep worry suffered these many years by her friends who had family in Europe. Japan had sided with Germany, had aided and abetted the hostile forces that caused all the wickedness. Why now should she find herself shocked at the type of punishment meted out to at least one of the gang? Had the populations in all the enemy countries not cooperated? Why should she feel sorry for them? Esther was well aware that, despite the relief and the thankfulness that the war itself had come to an end, dreadful tidings were about to arrive, tidings which would strike pain into every heart of the few hundred thousand Jews then in the country; and what of those who had survived the torment and the cruelty? Would this pain not affect their conduct, their handling of affairs for years to come?

These disturbing thoughts wearied her in spirit and body. She could not rejoice in the conquest of the evil when she visualized the suffering that would be the post-war lot of ordinary folk. Esther left the coffee cold on the table, the day's newspaper propped against the cup; she walked up and down the room, trying to sort out her feelings, to separate them from her thoughts.

Yes, she too had a fund of basic energy. She would use it constructively. On the morrow she would make an appointment with the contractor and discuss the building of her house.

* *
*

Ora goes to Germany

In accordance with her decision to work for the survivors of those unimaginable camps, Ora was sent for some months to a training center. Most of her time there was spent in packing parcels of food and clothing for despatch to the sufferers. She was also taught to drive, although she never needed to.

For, when she at last found herself in Germany with the Voluntary Jewish Relief Unit in the American Zone, she was driven around by one of the Displaced Persons she had come to help. It was these who needed to undergo the healing process of being made to feel necessary members of the human race.

Much later, Ora was asked about her journey to Germany. What was it like, what kind of emotion overtook her when she realized she was travelling to this hateful and hated country? The question embarrassed her, because she could not remember much.

Together with the other Jewish volunteers she queued up to board a rattling old vessel awaiting them in Newhaven. It was already overcrowded with soldiers. It was 10 p.m. on a winter night in 1946. Ora wondered where she was to sleep; she had never been on a ship before. But there were no sleeping arrangements. She roamed over the vessel until, below deck, she found a very uncomfortable deckchair in which she ensconced herself for the night. It was one of the worst nights she was ever to know. They did not sail until early the next morning, and the weather was bad enough even before the great storm that suddenly blew out of the sky and made everyone aboard violently sick. The ship rolled around in the heaving sea as if it were an empty, rotting old barrel.

Landing in Dieppe at last should have brought tremendous relief, but Ora was dazed and discouraged by her seasickness; she had always felt well by the sea and was a good swimmer, but now her head was too heavy to contain a single thought. Moving like a zombie, she took her place on the train that brought the group across France into the grayness of frozen Germany till it stopped somewhere in the American Zone. How many years have passed since Ora stepped off that train? Some fifty, probably. She still fails to understand how every detail of that train journey has vanished from her memory, even though she was "abroad" for the first time in her life.

She frowns, screws her face up till her strong features, her forehead, nose and mouth appear to merge into one solid piece of flesh.

She thinks and thinks but comes out again with the same statement that obviously surprises her as much as it does her questioner:

"I recall no detail of anything. No view from the window, no landscape, no realization that now and then we were passing through a town, as we must have done, no picture remains with me. I was simply in a daze."

"But when you saw railway lines running parallel with your train, did they not remind you of the horrible cattle trains that carried Jews, crowded and locked in, along those same lines rushing to hell?"

The reply is the same, with a shade of discomfort: "I remember nothing. I can't tell you anything about the train ride from Dieppe to Lampertheim."

Ah! At least the name has come back. Lampertheim. We'll look it up on the map. But Ora is not interested. It was just a village, why would it be on any map?

But Fräulein, being Fräulein, is insistent. One should know something about the place. She hauls out a volume of her ancient *Britannica* and turns the pages.

Such flimsy-seeming, almost transparent pages, so thin and so strong, untorn after almost a century of use. More than nine hundred pages in a volume take up barely an inch of shelf space. She turns the pages, wondering with half of her mind about the manufacture of such strong paper with the machinery then available, and is suddenly alert:

"I have it! Lampertheim," she quotes, "is a town in the Grand Duchy of Hesse-Darmstadt. Well, that reads fine enough," says Fräulein cynically, "a Grand Duchy. Germans and grandeur, of course. There is more, though. Just listen, Ora: 'Lampertheim has a Roman Catholic church.' Oh, great. Did they go there then for Confession after the Papal attitude to the Holocaust? But listen to this now: 'Lampertheim also has a fine Evangelical church.' Oh, and better still: 'Members of the Evangelical sect of Protestants give special prominence to the corruption of man's nature'!"

"I'm not sure what that means," wonders Fräulein, looking up from the page. "Does it mean they encouraged or were against the corruption of man's nature? The wording is strange."

"What a lot of rot!" Ora is her brisk self again. "I remember a village. Just a village with farming land around, and wooden houses. About a quarter of the place was taken over by a committee made up of the UNRRA, the Jewish Relief Unit, and the Joint American Distribution Committee. Duchies and churches, indeed!"

"What do you mean? A quarter of the place was taken over? How?"

Ora's memory is back, accurate and angry: "Many of the houses were made of wood, but were strong village dwellings of two storeys, and quite a few rooms on each floor. The Germans who were living in them were thrown out and told to find themselves accommodation elsewhere. After all the atrocities that these "pure" Aryans had committed, why should anyone have cared about them? The UNRRA took over a larger house for its own staff. The group of Displaced Persons in our care was housed in these emptied wooden structures."

Ora is silent again. One has to nudge her. Fifty years of buried memories. Who would want to recall the world of that period? She had been idealistic, naive. How could she at the time have had any true picture of what she would find in that world?

But one has to persist. It may appear unkind, but letting any detail be forgotten, even the smallest, seemingly most insignificant – that is equal to wiping it out as if it had not occurred. That is not permissible. So Fräulein persists:

"How old were these DPs you had to train?"

"Young enough. About eighteen or nineteen years old."

"And this chauffeur picked you up every morning and drove you to the farm?"

"My chauffeur. Yes, poor chap. He could drive all right, but he never kept his eyes on the road. On every trip his head would turn from right to left, from left to right. A zigzag driver!"

"That must have cost you nerves. What was it all about?"

"He was searching for his sister. They had been together in the Warsaw Ghetto, but in the upheaval of events had gotten separated. The poor chap was certain she was still alive, and he never stopped searching. He used to drive slowly, examining any female face he noticed on either side of the way."

What comment could one make?

* *
*

Vered finds solutions

We left Vered, newly widowed, attempting to manage life with her two young children. As the war drew to its close, the repulsiveness of the Nazi regime could no longer be treated as exaggerated rumor. For years the world had been shrugging off the notion that the people of Germany – Goethe's land, as they liked to say – had been countenancing the most hideous ugliness until it became a commonplace thing. But now no one with a conscience could remain indifferent to the hateful reality. It had to be faced, albeit unwillingly by some even to this day. In any case, there is no way by which the gruesomeness of that period can be explained or understood.

How should any ordinary person credit the information that millions of people had been destroyed, not in battle but in their very defenselessness? How imagine that innumerable human beings who had followed their simple routine of work and family were, after a certain date, transformed into living skeletons cooped up in huge barbed wire cages, and turned into a mockery of humanity devoid of all emotion save for a sense of hopelessness?

There are individuals who, when struck by shock, cannot utter a single word. Vered was one of these. The beating her husband had been given in Berlin had caused the internal injuries that, after some years of valiant labor to build a new life, had finally killed him.

The Kaiser's war in this same century had left Vered orphaned. She had now no one of her own kith and kin in Europe to mourn for. But, like Mrs. Kordovi, she was observant of the pain in the eyes of her neighbors, conscious of the agony in their hearts. She grieved silently, as deeply as those more directly involved. The aphorisms of her Old Lady were forgotten; any relevancy they may have had simply vanished. She became alive to events, avidly read the news-sheets published for German-speaking immigrants and suspected that, while the enemy had been vanquished, the guns silenced, yet peace was not about to accept the Jews of the Holy

Land in its embrace. Intuitively she knew that there was yet danger enough, and it would be closer to home. In February 1945 an Arab League had been founded. Vered did not delude herself that the Arabs, given the opportunity, would act more humanely than the Germans and the Japanese.

Her greatest fear was for her teenaged son. She would not allow his young life to be endangered – or worse – by the enemies in and surrounding this country. She vividly recalled her first sight of it in 1933 when she had been taken across the sand, seeing little more than thorns and thistles, mosquitoes and pests. It had all borne witness to a neglected, uncared-for small patch of the wide universe. Her husband, she and all the other Jews then in the country, they alone cared – and the results of the caring were apparent to anyone with an open mind. She would ensure her son's life as far as she could – even, terror-filled thought – even if it meant parting from him for a time. She would send him to England, where he could get the kind of schooling that would enable him to earn his bread in a suitable profession. By that time the unrest might have settled and he could come home.

The silent, unseen tears dampened her pillow the night after he had sailed. The memory of the Arab rioting that had lasted from 1936 until the outbreak of the Nazi war assured her she had done the best for her son.

In the morning she was calm and quiet, seeing her daughter off to school as usual. Vered walked around her empty house, from room to room. Then she walked around the large plot outside. She could still prepare the chicken feed, keep up the chicken run and sell the eggs. But that would hardly feed the two of them, let alone pay all other expenses. She had needed to outfit her son, pay his fare, provide him with some money. Without the help of some workmen, for which she could no longer pay, she could not look after the vegetable plots and the fruit trees that had so far brought in a small income. What now?

The donkey that had carried her husband daily to his orange grove had already been sold. The stable stood empty. She went in, looked around it seeing nothing, stood there like an automaton. The place had a kind of donkeyish smell about it still. She had never aired it; in her bereavement and worry she had completely forgotten such a task. Well, what difference did it make? She turned away, went out of the stable and fumbled for the key to lock the door.

And suddenly she awoke. She opened the stable door again and looked at it with different eyes. It was quite large; her husband had intended to buy two more donkeys for his children and had built the place accordingly. On one wall there was a tap. If she let out her roomy, white house, she would have an adequate income. The apathy fell away, her "basic energy" took over. A sink could be fixed just beneath the tap, a marble slab could be fitted on each side. The place needed whitewashing, the cement floor had to be tiled. Then a shower cubicle could be built adjacent to one corner of a wall.

A bed against each of two walls, a small table in the middle, a few chairs and a cupboard from the house – what more would they need? Vered even had a length of flowered cotton that would suffice for a curtain and a centerpiece for the table. A shelf for some books, a picture or two, and the place would be quite habitable.

It was all done in a couple of months, and she moved in with her daughter. So long as she had her child with her, life in the renovated stable was bearable. While the girl was at school, it took but a short time to clean out the place, to spread the chicken feed and collect the eggs that would be picked up later by the settlement truck.

And now she could allow herself what had been too great a luxury during all the years since she had come here: She could sit down with a book, could turn on the radio (the "wireless-set" had with American influence progressed to that title) and listen to the music she loved. Music had calmed our own moody King Saul, and, as Tennyson declared, lay gentlier on the spirit "than tired eyelids upon tired eyes." Vered's eyelids were tired enough.

Once a month she would look out for the postman bringing her a long, detailed letter from her son. With little pocket-money, he could not afford to write more often.

For the time being, Vered was content.

* *
*

Malka and the Purimspiel

Malka was less content. She was tired. With the loss of hope goes a certain loss of energy, and she now knew that her husband had been murdered by the Nazis. To the innumerable letters she had addressed to the International Red Cross in her attempts to locate her son, no clear reply had been received.

"Hoping and waiting leads only to prating," says a German proverb, freely translated. Malka endured her daily tasks, taking her half-day off as usual, but her motivation had weakened. Moreover, she was becoming too sensitive to the negative attitude of her non-Jewish employer.

Our Majestic Malka was working for Gentiles? How had that come about? In the 19th and 20th centuries, a German Christian sect known as the Templars, whose origins went far back to the Crusader period, built small settlements for themselves in various places in the Holy Land, for the avowed purpose of "realizing the apocalyptic vision of the prophets." The statement has rather a vague tone. It would be nice to know that what they had in mind was God's promise to His people through Isaiah (44:26):

> *It is I who say of Jerusalem*
> *"It shall be inhabited,"*
> *And of the towns of Judah*
> *"They shall be rebuilt."*

How ironic that these Templars had built "settlements" without arousing the world's opposition. Who ever dreamed that later, when the Holy Land was infused with the breath of Jewish life, was given legitimate recognition as the Jewish State, the word "settlements" would become something of a "dirty word," and the Jews who poured into the country – after suffering the torments of hell – would find themselves disparaged if they were known as "settlers"?

Well, but we are straying. In Haifa the Templars had built their solid, grayish houses along a broad way leading from the foot of the Carmel almost down to the sea. The way was known as "the German Colony." Each house stood in its own grounds, well planted with trees that offset something of the gray solidity. Over the door of each house a Biblical text had been engraved.

But gradually the numbers of the Templars dwindled. They were supposed to take monastic vows on joining the sect, which meant that there was no natural continuity. However, they had laid out a leafy straight thoroughfare, and although the façades of the houses looked rather gloomy, their large and roomy interiors made perfect homes for the many consulates stationed in Haifa during the Mandatory period.

It was in the household of one of these consuls that Malka had found work when she was desperate to be as fully occupied as possible. After the "affair of the onions" there were other silly incidents that were more annoying, were even hurtful, and gradually wore her down. Planning a formal dinner party, for instance, the consul's lady might tell her housekeeper:

"I think a tomato soup would be suitable – but don't give us one of your Jewish kinds."

Malka was an excellent cook, but too many first-class dishes were decried as "your Jewish stuff," while when the elegantly-clad diners had filled their glasses once too often, scornful remarks in slurred tones about "those Jews" would disclose the real opinions of these diplomats.

It happened too often that tall, well-built Malka, standing with the majestic mien that was natural to her, opposite her seated employer to "take orders" regarding the day's menu, would wonder to herself just where she really was. In her former home, in anti-Semitic Vienna, she had taken orders from no one. There she had been mistress of the household, while here, in her "own" country, she was employed by the kind of Jew-haters who had helped, if only by their attitude, to get her husband murdered.

The incongruity of it puzzled her. She did not yet know that any decision would be taken out of her hands, and that quite soon.

Just now, however, she was chatting with Fräulein, her faithful little friend:

"There is one thing in that house, though, that keeps me feeling pleasantly Jewish, and that is their *Purimspiel.*"

"Purimspiel? What are you talking about?"

"Well, but you'll hardly believe it. When the consul was transferred to Haifa from some outlandish little country in Africa, he brought his native valet with him. This person was here assigned the task of serving at table."

"So?"

"He is tall, rather dark-skinned, and he has to wear special clothes. I bet you've never seen such. He wears a colored, loose shirt and baggy trousers of black silk drawn in at the ankles with elastic. A wide cummerbund joins these two garments around the waist. Over this he wears a braided jacket with frogging around the buttonholes, and the entire costume is topped by a tall red fez with a black tassel bobbing and dangling as he moves. A real Purim costume."

Both women laugh. Malka's laughter is encouraging, one doesn't like to see this brave, hearty soul downcast.

"They have a funny, *goyishe* sort of little cake, very small, which they call 'skonns.' Also a name! Now, when they have afternoon tea, one of the servants makes these things. I have no recipe and never made such a cake or whatever it is."

Fräulein tried hard not to smile. She knew what scones were but had no recipe. She knew that Viennese Malka baked more sumptuously, and her portions would have been more generous. But let Malka tell on:

"These 'skonns' are counted, one to each guest, never more. The Purimspiel waiter holds out a brightly polished, very heavy tray, and the hot 'skonns' are placed on it. If there are only three guests, believe me, no more than three of these things will be put on this large tray. Then a very heavy oval cover, also brightly polished, is put on the tray to keep the 'skonns' hot; they may not be eaten cold, it seems.

"So imagine: This man in his Purim get-up goes carefully up the stairs from the kitchen, carrying the heavy tray stiffly before him. The silver is so bright, his clothes are reflected in it! He approaches each guest in turn, they sit around in the drawing-room, and in front of each guest the lid is lifted, for him or her to take a 'skonn.' If that is not a Purimspiel, I don't know what is."

But halt a second. Where are those village laborers of Vered's who rebelled at being given hot tea in the heat? One can imagine them crowding the consul's drawing-room and pointing a finger at "the naive girl who knew nothing of the world": "Ha, you told us there is no such thing as a Saloon society! Saloon, salon – what's the difference?" Indeed, little – when a drop too much has been imbibed...

Vered, too, would have found the scene amusing – though, perhaps, living in the donkey shed, she might have had a minute of pathos and old memories.

Well, but that's gone. All over. But did those dwellers in the Templars' "German Colony" never notice the rawness of the Land, and how it was coming to life? Were those consuls not representative of the wide world outside, even when they imbibed a drop too much?

Malka was tired of her job, tired of being made to feel inferior on account of her Jewish cooking, tired even of seeing the silliness of the Purimspiel.

But, as said, the decision was taken out of her hands. Beyond the consular kitchen, the world had the final say. With the outbreak of the war in 1939, many of the remaining 1,500 Templars were either repatriated or deported to Australia. And only a few years after the war's end, in 1948, the British Mandate also came to its end.

That the war might have been prevented made no difference; the destruction and the methods of killing had to be paid for. Governments had to reduce their expenses, and one after another the consulates were closed down. For a short time the houses remained shabby, uncared for. But then the State of Israel was opened up for every Jew wishful of "settling." Empty houses soon found inhabitants, and the "German Colony" was given a more suitable name.

Haifa found itself adorned with a beautiful, straight, leafy road. Malka went looking for other work.

* * *

A lady at her desk

"Dearest Ethel," writes Mrs. Kordovi to her daughter, "you cannot imagine my feelings just now. I am writing to you on my own desk, in my own small den, in my own large house! After all this time, it is actually built and I moved in a few days ago. People find it strange that I, a woman alone, should build such a spacious solid house just for myself. But your father would not have wanted it otherwise, and I am hoping that one day it will pass to my grandchildren. Perhaps they will even come and stay with me during holidays, as well as you and your brothers.

"Ethel, I wish I could describe the many discussions we had about its planning – the contractor, the architect, the engineer and I. It was no easy matter to build on this hard-baked, rocky ground. You will find no sign that anyone has trodden here since Rome conquered the country (except, of course, for that platoon of soldiers).

"Nor will you believe how many permits were required from so many offices, and how many forms and contracts I had to sign. It's amazing that anything in the way of building gets done at all, yet it does. At times I wonder whether the centuries of Talmud study, with its hair-splitting arguments and discussions, didn't get into our genes, making us so insistent on every dot and dash. And everything has to have its official stamp, and it all has to be overseen by a lawyer.

"Anyway, the house did get built. The debris is being cleared away, and then I shall see how the rough ground around the house can be turned into a proper garden. That was always our special hobby, Ethel, don't you remember?

"You will never believe this, my dear: There is no proper road from the town up here, the contractor could manage to get his laborers and the building materials up here with his truck. But me, how do you think I got up here almost daily for weeks and weeks? I got myself a donkey! Quite a clever one, too, it soon knew exactly the way up to the scaffolding.

"You should have seen my neighbors staring when they saw me put my bundles of curtains, towels and things in one panier, and some of my precious things of the old days in the other panier, and then saw me getting astride the animal! At first I took up large containers of water, because there were no pipes laid down or any other way of getting water."

Esther did not notice how long her letter was becoming. She liked to be in close touch with her children and usually put on paper all her thoughts, whatever she was writing about. She described her new house at length, she was so happy to have gotten away from the small rented place in town. Her friends would not visit her just yet, for they would not ride a donkey, but she doubted not that a bus service would be a fact one day. She felt like singing with the poet Browning:

"God's in his Heaven
All's right with the world."

But it wasn't and she knew it. What troubled Esther most was that, instead of one Jewish nation forming itself into a single body, she sensed that a split-up people was developing.

She was far from indifferent to the distress of friends who were learning what had happened to those whom they had left behind. She saw that individuals were withdrawing into themselves; the suffering scarred each separate soul. And when groups did come together, she had the feeling that the grouping set men apart more vigorously, Jews being emphatic and vociferously articulate in expressing their ideas.

It hurt her to hear those who altogether denied the God of Israel "who allowed this dreadful thing to happen. Why didn't He prevent it if all the power is His?"

Others would respond by recalling the testing of Daniel in the lion's den. Jews had survived so very much during the centuries, could they not stand up to this testing, dreadful as it had been? The nation was alive, even if greatly depleted.

Then there were those who rejected every form of Jewish life and tradition. It had brought them such a Holocaust, they declared, we need a different "philosophy" for the guidance of the country now in its rebirth: "Socialism in our day!" they proclaimed. So far as Mrs. Kordovi had given thought to fathoming this notion, she judged it meant that teachers, nurses, doctors – no matter what the responsibility that their work demanded – they should all earn about the same as the street sweeper. All that mattered was that every man should do his day's work, no matter how. But socialism was not her reason for coming to the Holy Land, and she did not study it further.

"The right to strike" was touted as inalienable and was freely exercised, too often and too much, causing as much trouble to those exercising this "right" as to those whose connection with its cause was non-existent. People's "rights" appeared to take on greater importance than their duties.

And at the other end of the philosophical pole were those who, fearing for the fate of Judaism altogether after the Nazi experience, made its laws more stringent, erecting a wall of intolerance in place of opening the door of outreach; thereby they distanced many who would in a more comfortable way have adhered to a milder version of their ancient faith. For with the stringency they were lost, and without a sympathetic, understandable form of Judaism, the special "personality" of the nation could be lost. The people were so bewildered by the terrible events of the past that a non-material element giving greater sensitivity to the meaning of life was vital.

All this and more Esther put into her letter. So much had been achieved, with such scanty means, she was anxious for her daughter to have the knowledge that would provide understanding. Esther could not bear to hear criticism of those who were formulating strange, un-Jewish notions because of the suffering that was overwhelming them.

"It is all so very interesting," she wrote, "I know you probably think I refer too often to what has befallen our people during our own lifetimes. But 'forgetfulness is like a forest in which men lose their way.' I don't recall who wrote that or if I am misquoting, but however it is put, it is true. If our nation, if the world, is allowed to forget, there will only be more suffering. What the outcome will be, none can say.

"But Ethel, dear daughter, we have been separated for so long. Do make plans to stay with me for a time. I want you so much to see this Jewish country. And especially I want you to see my house!"

Her wish was granted. When the State of Israel was proclaimed, Esther's heart was doubly moved; her daughter was at her side to share the incredible greatness of the marvel.

* * *

Ships in port

Approaching the shores of Palestine in July 1947 is a ship with "a pathetic load," as Dan Kurzman describes it in his book, *Genesis, 1948*. Crowded into this ship is a load of some four thousand five hundred Jews. Each of them had been through the pernicious evil of Hitler's attempt at a "Final Solution." Each of them had cause to point an accusing finger at mankind for the bitterness in their souls. Had their suffering, carried out so ruthlessly, been ignored? Connived? Or simply allowed to happen?

Their present desire was modest enough: to get out of this inhuman Europe, to go to the single place they could call "home," the one place to which they had a right. Both their haters and their own history had given them that right.

Earlier, in February of 1946, the Anglo-American Committee of Enquiry had expressed its view that "there was no place for Jews in Europe." The committee also declared it imperative to clear the Displaced Persons' camps. Judge B. Crum,* a member of the committee, had expressed his opinion that "the Jews have taken all the punishment they can. They are at breaking point."

One may wonder for a second at the use of the word "punishment." Judge Crum surely meant it in the sense that too much suffering had been inflicted on them.

Apparently the British Mandatory Power thought otherwise. The four thousand five hundred unfortunates would not be allowed to disembark in the land that the British had undertaken to develop as a Jewish National Home; the "passengers," despite their great need to make their exodus from any spot on the map of Europe, were put on three British frigates to be sent to Cyprus "or elsewhere," pending a decision on their future.

Nevertheless, ships with Jews in their holds did succeed in landing at various places along the coast of the Holy Land, whence their brother Jews smuggled them into and across the country. The Mandatory authorities branded them as "illegals," but the term was meaningless: Their forearms had long since been branded with numbers.

These "illegals," after regaining some measure of mental and physical health, took their full part both in the rebuilding of the country and in its defense. There was really nothing in the barren narrow stretch of land along the Eastern Mediterranean shore to arouse greed. But it had to be defended often enough, at great cost

---

* *Behind the Silken Curtain*, by Bartley Crum, published by Simon and Schuster

in life, against those who had no lack of spacious countries with their own religion, customs and language, in which to dwell and prosper.

Despite all, by the year 1949 the State of Israel, even though still in its infancy, was sturdy enough to offer hospitality to its own family. And the ship coming into the Port of Haifa today, in the spring of 1949, carried "legal" immigrants, though one could still have called them a "pathetic load."

Among the usual crowd in the harbor were a number of people we already know: Malka was there on the off chance that, perhaps, although no news of her son had reached her these many years, there might just be someone of hers alive and on that ship. She still remembered how she had sat on her suitcase in that very place, hearing the oft-repeated *"Lo yodéa"* and wondering where the Jews were. Technically she, too, was an "illegal" immigrant, having simply outstayed her term as tourist. She smiled as the knowledge suddenly struck her.

Then, too, there was the striking figure of Esther Kordovi who had come from Safed with her daughter Ethel, whose long-awaited visit to her mother had finally taken place and was almost at its end. There were also a number of social workers waiting there, as well as some kibbutz members. News had gotten around that there was a group of orphaned children on the ship drawing in. Some of the older ones had been taken out of the Displaced Persons' camps, while the younger ones, after years of being hidden from the barbarians who had orphaned them, had now been brought "home." How many times have we used that word "home" in these pages, and how many different pictures has the word evoked!

With Malka was the quiet Fräulein to whose care some of the smaller orphans were to be committed.

Ethel, as tall and impressive-looking as her mother, had been amazed at her mother's achievement. She had never imagined that such a fine house and such a beautiful little garden could have "grown" out of the uncared-for ground her mother's letters had described. She wanted now to see for herself the return of Jews to their homeland, to greet them, to express something of her deep emotion. She would take the imprinted memory back to England.

Also, the idea had crossed her mind that, possibly, one of the older girls coming off that ship could go home with Esther, so that her mother would have a companion, while the parentless girl would be well cared for. But that did not work out, arrangements had been made for all the immigrants, young and old.

A wagonload of toys awaited the children who now came down the ramp in a state of bewilderment. Too much had happened in their young lives, events without rhyme or reason. The children hardly knew what the toys were or what to do with them. Like Jane Eyre, they had little experience of such things. What, however, did catch their interest was the huge cake that Esther Kordovi and her daughter Ethel had brought along and now placed on a ledge of old wall. A great oblong of pastry had been iced with colored marzipan, chocolate and a variety of sweetmeats in such a fashion that the cake looked like a real house and garden in *bas-relief*. Actually, it was a replica of the house on the hilltop that was the self-designed home of Mrs. Kordovi.

Malka moved around slowly among those disembarking. Faint as her hope had been, she knew that in reality she had nothing to hope for, at least not this time. But other ships would be coming. She could not know that when the right ship did arrive, she would be confined to a hospital bed.

She walked now, with her majestic mien, across the quay to see what had attracted the interest of the hitherto apathetic children. Turning to the elder of the two ladies standing by the cake, she said, with Fräulein as interpreter:

"Well, I have baked many fine tortes and pastries in my time, but never anything as beautiful as this."

"My daughter Ethel, here, it is her work. I only baked the dough, but she made it look like my house."

Her friendly tone encouraged Malka to further praise the sugar and chocolate construction and to ask Ethel the reason for it. No one knew better than Malka the patience and artistry that such a result demanded.

"These children," replied Ethel, "have never known the beauty of home. I wanted to be the first to give them an idea of it."

"I remember," said Malka slowly, as the memory came back, "how my grandfather told me that when he and his friends were sent to the *Heder* for the first time to begin learning our holy Torah, the *Melamed* would give them honey to lick as he taught the first letters, so that Torah learning would always be associated with the taste of sweetness. I think your delicious-looking cake was made on the same principle."

Esther and Ethel exclaimed in surprise. Being females, they would not have been sent to *Heder*. Nor had they, in Singapore, known of a *Heder* or a *Melamed* (teacher of Hebrew). Twice weekly a Rabbi had come to the house to teach the girls their prayers. In fact, Malka's own father in Vienna had acted likewise, and in her youth Malka had found it very boring, especially as she had not been taught the meaning of the strange script that read from right to left. She now bid the two ladies good-bye, saying to Fräulein as she walked away:

"What lovely ladies!"

And they said about her: "What a nice person that is!"

Like ships that pass in the night.

The children meanwhile were still gazing with wonder at the lovely structure of house and garden made of chocolate and marzipan, unknown ingredients to them. Watching them, Ethel thought she would cut the cake and give each child a goodly slice. She was shocked and surprised when the youngsters, seeing her approach with knife ready to cut, called out practically in unison:

"No! No! Please don't spoil the pretty house!"

She looked up, puzzled. Then the adult in charge of the group came up and explained softly: "These children have been kept alive by means of wiles, secretly, and in great austerity. It could not have been otherwise. They don't know what cake is, they have never seen or eaten any."

By this time the buses had arrived and the young folk had to be sorted out according to the arrangements made for them.

The cake was covered with silver foil and placed very carefully in one of the cars.

But Ethel could not credit what her ears had heard; it was impossible, how could it be true?

"Children! Small children who have never eaten a bit of cake!"

Her voice echoed that sentence in her mind all the way back to England.

* *
*

Scene in a café

Her head slightly bent, her stride less purposeful, Malka walked across the road from the harbor to her bus stop. Watching her, Fräulein ran and caught up with her:

"There is a small café just along the road; we are both tired, and I, for one, shall drop if I don't get a cup of coffee."

Malka smiled. She knew her little friend.

"*Na ja,*" she agreed, "we've been standing so long. It was so awful to see those little children; they lost their parents, they lost their years of infancy. How will they turn out?"

"They are among their own, they'll be looked after. Now, will you have a cup of coffee with me or must I go alone?"

Over the coffee, the younger woman deliberately began to chatter.

"Yesterday, at the hairdresser's, I was sitting next to this woman, and she never stopped talking. She was telling me about her mother-in-law – and, believe it or not, she loved her! She kept saying what a wonderful person she was, so good to her, no one could tell that she was not her own, but her husband's mother. She had invited her to dinner, that was why she was having her hair done, and she wanted to look really nice."

"Well?" asked Malka, for the prattle had suddenly stopped. Too late, Fräulein was inwardly scolding herself for a tactless fool. Fancy her, of all people, saying anything that might remind Malka of her own unknown daughter-in-law! But Malka asked again: "Well, so?"

There was no help for it, she had to go on with the story:

"There was this problem, the mother-in-law was kosher, while this young woman was not. But having given the invitation and prepared a fine meat stew, she could not draw back. So she went to the kosher butcher, bought a fresh piece of kosher meat, tied a bit of string around it and placed it in the pot of stew. She was sure her mother-in-law would be pleased when, after the string was removed, she would explain that she had made her a special piece of kosher meat."

Malka laughed, remarking on the ignorance of the young bride, but admitted that one could not find many young women today so intent on showing esteem and affection for a mother-in-law.

Fräulein hastened now to change the subject and rushed on with another story: She had once stayed at a bed-and-breakfast place abroad. Among the many guests there was a family from Israel, apparently grandparents with two young grandchildren. Among all the other languages spoken in the dining room, their Hebrew was loud and distinct.

The breakfast buffet was laid out with a luscious array of various dishes that included not only many kinds of cheese, but a choice of cold meat cuts, sausages and the like.

"It's not polite to look at another person's plate," declared Fräulein, "so I don't know what they took, but obviously the place was not kosher. However, after they had gone around the buffet and filled their plates, they stood around their table. Then the grandfather took a skull-cap out of his pocket, placed it on his head and said Grace in Hebrew, after which he replaced the cap in his pocket and motioned to his family to sit down and eat their breakfast."

"*Kol hakavod*,"* responded Malka, "he wasn't ashamed of his Jewishness before all those *goyim*."

That had not been the point of the story, thought Fräulein, but she did not wish to argue about principles that morning. She merely commented that Jews can be very strange people. But Malka also had a story to tell. She had perked up a bit. After the experience in the port that morning, to sit and chat was just what she needed.

"Did you ever meet Mrs. Michelle?" asked Malka. "She does some sewing for us occasionally. Her family, she told us, had lived in Lebanon for generations – possibly it was one of her ancestors who had served as intermediary when cedar wood had to be purchased for the First or Second Temples in Jerusalem." (Historical imagination is a wonderful asset!) "Her father sensed that, in this twentieth century, the atmosphere was changing and they might need to move on; therefore he resolved that all his children, not merely the sons, be educated for a different kind of life. He decided that only at the French Convent School would his daughter achieve literacy and also learn sewing or some handiwork that would be useful in hard times. But, you know, even a clever man, one with some foresight, isn't always entirely wise. Our Mrs. Michelle was about eleven or twelve years old when she was placed in the nuns' boarding school. She was not very happy there, but her father would listen to no complaints.

"However, one day in the last week of December, the child suddenly arrived home, carrying her suitcase.

"'What is the matter?' asked her father sternly.

She explained that all the pupils had been sent home for Christmas.

"'What have you to do with Christmas? It is not our holiday,' was her father's stern response. 'Back to school with you at once!'

---

* *Kol hakavod* (literally, "All Honor") = "Good for him" or "More power to him"

"Crying did not help the girl, she had to take up her case and return to the Convent, the only Jewish girl spending Christmas with the nuns."

Weeping had not helped the child – but laughter is its own healing process, and Malka went to the bus stop then with something of her usual upright gait.

And you, Mr. Thackeray, of Vanity Fair fame, what philosophy or crumb of cogitation could you or other non-Jews have gotten from listening to this Jewish prattle?

Could a story be woven from ideas rather than from the interaction of people?

* *
*

Ora in a scene of distortion

Ora was urged: "Tell about your own work in the Lampertheim camp. That should not be so painful."

"I taught them farming," Ora replies. "Not so painful? I'm not sure about that, I don't think I was very successful."

"Why not? You were a Land Army girl, and you loved the work." Ora gives a kind of sigh. How can one make outsiders understand? It had nothing at all to do with loving the work. But she seems to have let herself in for digging up these old memories. So be it.

"These young persons, having been 'displaced,' wanted only one thing: to get out of Europe. They detested even the sound of the name. Nor is there an authentic meaning to the word 'displaced' in this context. Children and adolescents were torn out of their accustomed environment; they were not asked for their consent. They were put through the torments of gehenna, they were brutalized, tortured. Then one day it is over, they are sent somewhere else, they don't know why, where, how; they don't know what had happened to their parents, sisters, brothers, school pals. And they are given a name: Displaced Persons."

Ora shrugs. The world must know? Someone asks and wants an answer? One had the feeling she would rather like to scream, at the top of her voice: "Shut up! Stop it. No one cares. They didn't then, and they don't now."

But she is quiet, controlled. Her voice is the same as usual. She goes on: "They wanted to go to Palestine. They had an atavistic memory of Palestine as the home of the Jewish People. They wanted nothing more than to go home. That's a simple enough wish, isn't it?

"We're talking about 1946, 1947. There was no State of Israel yet, and there was very little industry in Palestine at the time. So they were to be prepared for a life in agriculture.

"The first thing I did, or tried to do, was to teach them how to milk cows. But for this they had to be up very early in the morning, before dawn. It was winter, still dark at 5 a.m., and icy cold.

"The powers-that-be, discussing ways and means in their warm conference room, decided that this regimen of rising early to go to work would strengthen the young folk, would accustom them to a routine, and this would make them fitter, both mentally and physically.

"But the DPs resented it after all the hardships they had undergone. Had they ever been allowed a late morning in a warm bed? It seemed to them that the hatefulness of what had been their lives so far was merely being continued, if in a more humane way.

"Then, you must understand, the farm really belonged to a Nazi. More than anything, they hated having, as they thought, to work for him. And, to be honest, that Nazi's expression was not the pleasantest. One can imagine his thoughts when he saw young Jews coming daily onto his land. And there was no way these DPs could be convinced that they were working for their own good; they were not working *for* him, he was just being made use of.

"They had never milked cows before; when they saw him watching, always standing there with his arms akimbo, and his angry red face, they would not exert themselves.

"I tried to encourage them by telling them how fine it would be for them to arrive in Palestine as expert landworkers. But they said: 'First let's get there, then we'll see.' Meanwhile the cows were beginning to dry up. The milk would not flow in response to weak fumbling fingers."

Ora is silent again. Then she makes a strange remark:

"It was all one great distortion."

Puzzled, one can only look at her. She is patient:

"Daily, that Nazi would grumble about the damage to his farm and his cows. But he wouldn't complain openly to the Americans, he was afraid of them. Our Jewish tyros could not bear to see his disapproving visage, he was always watching them, but their own past experience had told them that they had no one to complain to about his presence there. They were glad, even, that their 'work' was causing him damage, and they refused to exert themselves.

"But I had to induce those youngsters to learn the task and do it properly. Those were my orders from above. And while I understood the DPs, I at the same time hated feeling ineffectual. I was afraid my superiors would be dissatisfied with me – and I was afraid of that Nazi just because he was a Nazi! Nor had I forgotten the farmer's wife back in England, nor that German prisoner of war.

"After all these years, perhaps it seems like a huge joke. After all, the war was over, the Nazis were beaten – they were like drenched curs. And we Jews had not been completely wiped out as the Germans had hoped. They saw us there daily, in the village they had had to themselves.

"Yet we were all still afraid. They of us and we of them. That was the distortion."

The interviewer tries to state matters more succinctly:

"But there was an acknowledged goal: to get to Palestine. Didn't that become an ideal, an aim, no matter what?"

Ora sees that she has not expressed herself clearly: "Ideals? Who even knew there was such a word? Ideals were no part of the immediate post-Nazi period. These young Jews had struggled simply to remain alive. Today was possible only because of yesterday's struggle. 'Tomorrow' was a meaningless term of speech. Ideals! How much idealism is there in today's world? Is the word still in use anywhere?"

It is too much to take in. Whoever fights wars has to win, that was so from the beginning of time. They used words like "glory," "honor," "homage to heroes" and so on – but it was all just killing, shedding blood.

Ora is right. Perhaps one should get away from delving into such depths of human activity. Is there nothing pleasant at all? After all, the DPs had survived, and the nation of Jews had not been obliterated. A question comes to mind:

"What happened to your zigzag chauffeur? Did he find his sister?"

"Yes, he did – but I'll tell you of that another time. I'm tired."

So rest awhile, Ora. One cannot unearth so much hatefulness all in one go.

* * *

More hurt for Vered

Her son's monthly letters made more cheerful reading than the daily newspapers. He was making excellent progress, life in England was good, even with the rationing and the clothing coupons. The people were nothing like those officials of the Mandatory Power in Palestine.

Eventually the young man built a life for himself in England. With the passing of the years, the memory of the sandy little village where his mother and sister were became ever fainter. One day, he would be, like his generation "too busy" to do much more for them than send good wishes at Festival times.

But that was still in the future, and Vered was content to know that her son was far from the danger threatening this small "Holy Land." For the end of the war in Europe and Japan had not brought peace to our own narrow strip of land. It was but a poor strip, indeed, with few natural resources.

But greed, envy and power-lust, in the guise of religious fervor, form their own initiative. Rioting and killing were the order of the day.

The United Nations proposed a plan of partition: Arab and Jew would live each in his officially determined enclave. But the Arabs refused. In response to the proposal, they killed a hundred and twenty-six Jews in a violent onslaught during the last fortnight of 1947 alone.

No one could now expect Jews to remain passive, not after Nazism. Those days had gone.

The Jew-haters of Europe, the callously indifferent world community, the Holocaust deniers – they were the very people who raised the type of Jew who would defend himself and his brethren, would give as good as he got – and more if necessary.

So it was natural that Vered's heart was at rest when she knew her son was far away. But that her daughter could be in danger had not crossed her mind. Vered had not marked the passing of time. In 1933 she had brought a couple of infants to the country, a boy of six or seven, a girl of four or five. And now it was 1947. Probably her daughter had been given a proper name, but as with Fräulein, no one knew it. Vered invariably spoke of the child as *Seelchen* – Little Soul. When her schooling ended and Seelchen's eighteenth birthday arrived, the young lady made her own decision: she joined the *Haganah*, the Jewish defense force that, after Independence, became the official Israeli army. Seelchen was away from home for long weeks at a time, sending messages through friends to reassure her mother. Came the day when, alone in her "residence" (she was living in the donkey shed, remember?), Vered received an unexpected message. Her beloved daughter, her Seelchen, was among the group of Jewish soldiers captured by the Jordanians when the Old City of Jerusalem fell. The Old City that had since King David's day been the capital city of Judah, and that Jews the world over had mourned for since

Rome had conquered her. Nevertheless, devastated as the city was, devoid of her legendary beauty, Jews had gone back to dwell within her walls. Crowded into her narrow alleys, there had been a population of 40,000 Jews, 7,000 Moslems and 13,000 Christians living there in 1905, according to the 1911 edition of the *Encylopaedia Britannica*. What claim could any other nation have to the Old City of Jerusalem?

But Vered had no thought of any of this. She knew only that her Seelchen was not among Jews anymore. As was Vered's nature when stunned, her lips quivered, but no sound emerged. At least, not at that moment.

A few days later, someone knocked on Fräulein's door, a kind of bashful, hesitant knock. It was Vered. Her silver hair was more windswept than usual, the whiteness of her face accentuated by the black rings around her eyes. She sat there quietly for awhile, her lips making, every few seconds, a soundless movement. She needed to talk. She didn't know how. She could not make herself articulate the mixed-up pain; she was afraid to hear it aloud from her own voice.

But of course it came out because it had to:

"When I got the message that my Seelchen is in captivity, my world turned over. I might have been back in Nazi Germany. I think at that moment I almost lost my sanity. It must have been the smell of the donkey, the place reeked of it. I thought I would die if I did not get another kind of air to smell."

Her eyes, once so full of ready laughter, had that look of pain that belongs wholly to mothers. There is no other hurt like that.

Minutes pass, there is no point, no humanity in pressing her to continue. She must take her time. When she does speak again, her voice is brittle, her sentences abrupt:

"I had to get away from the smell of that donkey," she assures her companion, "but I did not know where to run. I opened the door and stood there. Then something terrible took hold of me. I started to scream. The first time in my life. I screamed and screamed. My voice cracked, my throat hurt. I came to myself. I went inside again."

Perhaps now one can give her a word of comfort: "They won't hurt the girls. Soon there will be a truce, and all the prisoners will be freed. You'll see, Seelchen will come home safe and sound." She did, too. But Vered has hardly listened. Comfort is not on her agenda just now. Her face has become even more ashen, if that were possible.

"An hour later," she continues, "a neighbor knocked on my door. The one who looked after the orange grove when my Aryeh died, if you remember. He told me that I was to go with him to Haifa the next day. That was yesterday. He had seen me there in the doorway, he must have heard me screaming, his house is just a plot away. I understood not a word of what he was saying, just looked at him – probably very foolishly. But he said again quietly: 'Get ready to come to Haifa with me in the morning.' Probably he did not want to make me feel ashamed of myself for having been noticed in such a state."

One could only think silently: "Bless you, unknown neighbor, bless you for your sensitivity."

Vered hesitates for just a second. But she is too honest. There is not even a hint of self-defense nor of defiance in her tone; she speaks quietly, factually:

"So he called for me yesterday morning and we took the bus to Haifa. We lunched at a restaurant overlooking the Haifa Bay, and we sat there till the lights began to come on, and the whole city was twinkling. I could not make conversation. My mouth was dumb. Then he said he had booked a room for us at the Panorama Hotel."

Vered is quiet for a fraction of a second, then continues in the same tone, low and factual:

"We have been neighbors all the years, since the first houses went up in the village. Sometimes one's blood speaks. We spent the night in the hotel. But a woman can go only once to the Panorama Hotel.

"He took the bus back to work this morning, and I came to you."

Only once, dearest Vered? Before the Nazis, your husband took you to the finest hotels in Europe, you loved travelling, and you both enjoyed attending theater and opera performances. But here, only once can you be taken to the Panorama Hotel – once, when your heart is at breaking point.

Vered's hair is silver, her skin parched by the sun, there are lines in her face where none should be – for the whole little woman is barely two or three and forty.

And anyone with her at this particular moment of her life may be as morally prudish as any nun, but there is no preventing the thought:

"Bless you again, good neighbor of hers. You helped her to become a whole feminine woman – instead of a creature howling in pain."

"Come home with me," said Fräulein.

And after a few weeks of rest in an atmosphere of friendship, Vered got ready to leave.

"I shall rent a room in Jerusalem and find some kind of job. When my Seelchen is released, it will be in Jerusalem, and I shall be there waiting for her. We will not return to the donkey shed, not ever again."

Nor did they.

* *
*

Farewell, Esther Kordovi

Esther was full of praise for the God of Israel. Daily she would declare, in the words of generations before her:

"...How goodly is our portion, how pleasant our lot,
How beautiful our heritage..."

She had built herself a home in the Holy Land of the People of Israel; the cruel war in Europe was over; her daughter had paid her a long visit – oh! the pleasurable weeks they had spent after a separation of years. And to crown it all, she and her daughter had witnessed the arrival of little children, the Jewish children who had escaped the fate marked out for them and were now frolicking in childish joy and human freedom in their own country.

Though no longer as young as she might have wished, she yet worked daily in her garden, bending her back over the soil to ensure its blossoming in a great burst of color. Her trees were growing tall and strong and green.

When she saw her flowers open to the sun in the mornings, a mass of orange and mauve and yellow and white and red, in their green framework of grass and hedge, she felt that this was her real thank-offering, that the good God in His Heaven was looking down with unalloyed bliss on the beauty she had created with His help.

The rooms of Esther's house were high and spacious, and the wide windows showed the landscape as if each window were a framed painting by one of the world's finest painters. Mrs. Kordovi corrected herself as she looked out: the world's Finest Painter, its Creator.

The idea gave her a thought: It was too far for her to walk down to the synagogue on Shabbat and then walk up again. And certainly she could not use the donkey on the Day of Rest. She had attempted the walk when she had first moved into her house, but it had been too much for her. The problem was easily solved. She had a small prayer room built against one side of her house. And within a very few years a few painters, attracted by the vista, built cottages in the vicinity, so that there were neighbors for sociability. And then there came Jews who invested in the erection of a comfortable hotel. The cool summers, the "Great Painter's" surroundings, assured the hotel's popularity. Staff was needed for the hotel, more cottages were built to house the employees, a bus service came into action.

The prayer room was open to all and before long became a beautiful little synagogue. On Shabbat and Festivals it always had more than the necessary ten men, despite the smallness of the neighborhood.

Now and again, some unrecognized young man would visit Esther, asking:

"Don't you remember me? I was in uniform then, but I often made *Kiddush* for you in that little flat you had down in town."

Sometimes the young man had come to settle, sometimes sentiment and plain curiosity had brought him to visit this new Jewish State, to see how it was turning out. One such visitor brought her a large sprig of lilac from his English garden, and she planted it in the shade of a hedge. In the coolness of this northerly hilltop it would grow; it might really flourish even in this different climate and poor soil.

And Esther was content. Perhaps too much so; one may not expect full measure, for it is not given. Like Vered, she too received an unexpected message: Her daughter was gravely ill.

There was no thinking, no deliberating as had been the case when Benedict died. She thrust into a bag her nightwear, her toothbrush, a change of underwear, her long-unworn heavy coat. Then she called for a taxi. She did not stop to look back at her house and garden, but at the last minute she ran to her desk and took out her long-lapsed British Colonial passport.

It was already possible to travel by plane; she knew her sons would wait for her at the London airport. But getting out of that place was not so simple. Finally she asked to see someone in authority and was confronted by a tall, uniformed man with very shrewd eyes. He was astonished to hear this old lady, her carriage still queenly, her clothes less so, her English not merely perfect but cultured in tone and expression, saying to him authoritatively – no, she did not plead, she told him:

"I must go to see my sick daughter. I don't know how long I need to be here, but I promise you, when it is time for me to go,

I shall ask for you; then you may fine me or put me in prison or quarantine – punish me in any way you see fit. But now, this minute I am walking out of here; my sons are waiting to take me to my daughter, nobody will stop me!"

He let her go, merely retaining her lapsed passport.

"This funny newcomer from heaven knows where," as the Safed grocer had defined her, sat at her daughter's bedside. She soon understood that Ethel had been aware of her hopeless illness and had made the journey to Safed to give her mother a daughter's companionship as long as it was possible.

Esther felt humbled. She had been too satisfied with herself and her occupation, but the real heroine was her Ethel, lying there now so shrivelled, so obviously in pain, but looking at her mother with eyes of love.

"Did the children enjoy the cake, mother?" she asked, and Esther assured her that they had loved it.

"Fancy making a world, mother," murmured the weak voice, "where small children never get anything sweet and don't have toys to play with."

Ethel closed her eyes. She was at peace.

When the week of mourning was over, Esther took leave of her sons and in the airport searched out the official, as she had promised. He himself escorted her onto the plane, asking that she be well looked after on the journey.

Back in her house on the hilltop, Esther occupied herself as usual. She now engaged a girl to help with the housework, her synagogue was kept bright and inviting, her garden blossomed, and even the lilac thrived. She blessed God for it all, in her customary way.

As often happens, however, acquaintances were embarrassed, they didn't know how to greet her, which words of comfort to use. There is no comfort for any mother who loses a child of her womb.

But bowls of soup and other comestibles appeared in her refrigerator, as if of their own accord – and stayed there. When

Esther remembered that she was hungry, she cut a slice of bread from what was often a very stale loaf.

One autumn afternoon, Fräulein, now, too, so much older, came up to visit the old lady. Always hospitable, Esther searched her pantry; it was so long since she had had real visitors. She found a small bowl of stewed fruit, so old that it had fermented, but she did not know that. She put a pretty lace cloth on a tray, added a spoon to the dish and set it in her friendly way before the guest. And the guest thanked her hostess and ate, allowing no hint of the food's bad taste to reveal itself. The day waned, and it began to grow dark. Fräulein thought Esther would feel cosier if the curtains were drawn, but was deterred:

"Oh, no," said Mrs. Kordovi, "see how my trees are nodding to me." A wind was blowing up, the trees were swaying and the old lady said lovingly: "See, it is time for evening prayers."

So Fräulein took her leave, knowing that this pious lady would prefer to pray alone these days. And not long after that, neighbors gathered to mourn and pray for this gentle, heroic old soul.

* * *

Ora and a scene of fire

All sorts of memories crowd her brain now. Ora is finding it hard to put first things first, each episode in its right place. Perhaps it would be simpler to paint, then the entire jumble could find space on the one broad canvas. After examining such a picture, Munch's "The Scream" might even come as an anti-climax.

"I told you about the wooden houses," Ora recalls, "they had probably been built specially for the farm laborers. In each of them, in the middle of the floor, there was a heating stove that rose through a hole in the ceiling to heat the upper story as well. It was winter, and cold enough. If you remember, I told you that some of the older DPs were given specific tasks. One of these tasks was to light the stove every evening just before the young folk came back from the farm. Do you remember the lamp-lighter of our childhood days in London?"

Who wouldn't? Such a pleasant, nostalgic memory. How can things change so utterly within the space of a single lifetime? Not even that, we still had some years to go.

"Well, one evening, this stove-lighter was late. The girl living upstairs had gotten home before him and was shivering with cold. She thought she'd try to light the thing herself. I don't believe she had ever done it before and didn't really know how, but she tried anyhow. She needed some warmth.

"I don't know just what she did," says Ora, "but something went wrong and the stove blew up. Before anyone noticed the smoke and could get to the house, it was all in flames, and the girl could not be saved. You can imagine the shock we were all in!

"Then this peasant woman, who had lived there before we took it over, came running across, mad with rage, shouting that we had burnt her house down.

"That a young woman had been burnt alive did not bother her in the least. Of course, the directress of our camp gave her the thoroughly furious scolding she deserved. It was so horrible. I know what it means to have one's house burnt down – but a house can be rebuilt; a human being, once dead, cannot be brought to life.

"I often wonder," remarks Ora, "whether that burnt young woman was counted among the six million? It's easy to say she should have waited for the man to come and do his job – but whoever thinks that way has never felt frozen to his guts."

As patiently as to a child, Ora makes another attempt to explain her concept of the "distortion" she had spoken of. In the newspapers, to the world, the war was over, the beastliness was done with. People could get on with rebuilding their bombed cities and normalizing their lives.

"But we were involved in a different way. We were making our feeble efforts 'to pick up the pieces,' as it were, and we were still in the midst of the horror."

And, as Ora recalls it, even this horror was sometimes just silly.

"The Americans (in whose zone we were working) had laid down a strict rule of non-fraternization. There was not to be the slightest hint of anything remotely resembling kindness in our attitude towards the Germans. We could not disagree with that. It was undeniable that they deserved no kindness.

"One aspect of this non-fraternization was prostitution. From time to time, the non-Jewish camp director would send inspectors from house to house to make certain that no easy lady of the night was earning some pennies by giving her services. Such inspections took place after midnight, when every inmate should have been asleep in his or her own room. But on a few occasions the inspector found a man and a woman together and would make a fuss.

"I had my work cut out to make the inspector understand that this had nothing to do with prostitution. These were young Jews, living in the same house or in the group of houses, who had been through unimaginable suffering. They had lost their families, everyone who had belonged to them. They were hungering for human warmth and closeness. Perhaps they were only in their late adolescence, but in experience of life they were far too mature for their years. After all that had been taken from them in their young lives, were they now to be deprived of the freedom to feel human? Were they expected to live as if in a monastery or convent?"

Ora had a hard time explaining this. After all the brutality, how could their terrible need for human affection be considered immoral? What connection did the coming together of a young Jewish couple have with non-fraternization? The couple may even have been intent on marrying once they got away from the place.

How could responsible adults have been so silly?

People are silly; that's an easy answer!

Her companion reminds her that she was going to tell about her zigzag driver, and Ora smiles. It seems a pleasant memory has come. Yes, her driver – did we not give him the title of "chauffeur"? – he actually did find his sister. There were a few similar DP camps within the area allotted, and at Ora's suggestion, he had driven around from one to the other – until in one camp he saw his sister. Ora will say no more of the meeting than that "it was very emotional."

At her driver's request, she went to visit his sister; she describes the camp:

"It was hateful. Horrid old barracks had been divided into small compartments by means of ragged old lengths of material hung up every few meters. The place was ice-cold, there were no heating arrangements. It was very long, and right at the end there was a door with the letters 'W.C.' painted up in white.

"I do not know how to describe this to you," says Ora. "You have asked me for a true picture of DP camp conditions; there is no way I can embroider the truth. Behind that door there were no toilets, there was a wide, long floor, and it was covered entirely with a thick layer of excrement. When nature called, people simply went in and answered the call. When I visited, it was winter, so the floorful of muck was deep-frozen, one could not tell how many layers had been frozen over.

"I tried to exert what little authority or influence I had – I was also in uniform, you know – and I tried to get them to clean the place out. But the inmates had all come from concentration camps, they were so inured to inhuman conditions that they simply did not care!

"Don't you find it unnatural that so little outcry was made at this utter debasement of human beings? No one appears to know anything about what it was like inside these DP camps."

There is an answer to this charge, an answer, though no defense: "People want to forget. They don't want to hear anything more about Hitler's war or even about the Holocaust. They don't want to read about it or hear about it. Today's world is intent only on making money and having fun."

"So why am I telling you all this?" she asks, reasonably enough. To this, too, there is an answer, a valid one: "It must all be recorded. Otherwise it will vanish from the world's memory as if it had never happened."

"Then let me finish, at least as much as I can remember. Someone at the top must have decided that I was not strict enough with my charges; they made little progress with their farm work and, after a time, were left to their own resources. I was transferred to a children's summer camp at Lindenfels. About three hundred Jewish children, many of them tiny tots, were sent to regain health and strength in this part of Germany. You may think this was a pleasanter task for me. But I felt that the transfer reflected on my inability to be stern with the farmworkers entrusted to me."

In fact, being stern was not in Ora's make-up at all. The Germans had been more than hateful. There is no word that describes their attitude. They deserved their downfall. They deserved more punishment than they got. Nothing could have been harsh enough.

But, unfortunately for her, Ora's basic kindness could not look on unconcernedly when she saw poor German peasants being bullied. They were so obviously a defeated nation, and they used to hide whatever they could. But the DPs got wise to this and would force the farmers to open up any hiding place discovered and hand over the contents of the cache.

"Let's leave it for now," Ora suggests. "I went out as a relief worker. I had some idea of doing good; but when I found myself helpless, unable to exert a beneficial influence, when I understood that correct behavior was seen by those unfortunates as plain silly – well, that was not a world I could find my way in."

Next time, then. But recorded it must be, little or much, meaningful or trivial.

* *
*

Change of scene for Malka

Malka took her time in looking for work; she was ready for something more satisfying than housekeeping. On learning of the death, alone in her house, of Esther Kordovi, Malka decided it would suit her to look after elderly, infirm citizens in a Senior Citizens' Home (a sympathetic euphemism for "Old Age Home"!). An obviously energetic and sensible woman, she soon found work in such a Home and was happy with her decision. It enabled her to put to good use the great warmth of heart that was her natural birthright. The old folk enjoyed her Viennese humor, she uttered a kind word here, gave a helping hand there, soothed many a parent whose children did not visit so often; after all, the parent was now taken good care of in the Home, no? There was plenty for Malka to do.

And if there were no problems with onions or tomato soup, there were other puzzling items she had never thought about. One old man, for instance, had received a gift: a few pairs of brand new socks. Proudly, he showed them to everyone – what good children he had! But the days of suspenders had long passed and modern socks have elasticized tops which hurt the calves of his legs.

What to do? What to do? One cannot simply cut off the tops. They would be too short, those fine, new socks, and they would no doubt wriggle down to form "bagels" around his ankles. Malka took the problem to her friend Fräulein, who had a ready solution, not even needing a Book of General Knowledge!

"Heat kills rubber," she informed Malka. "Stretch the tops under a very hot iron."

Patching a very old tablecloth was more difficult. One inmate, married sixty years earlier and now widowed, possessed a fine damask tablecloth that had been part of her trousseau. She would never use it, intending it as an heirloom for her granddaughter. But to keep it white, she washed it now and then – and one day discovered a small hole in the precious relic. Naturally, she brought it to Malka, insisting that it be invisibly mended, so that no flaw would be noticeable in the beautiful, intricate pattern of the cloth.

But neither Malka nor Fräulein could solve this problem. Invisible mending might be done by a tailor on tweed or worsted – but a fine old damask tablecloth, that was something else. The hole could be neatly darned or patched, but either way the repair would be visible.

Poor Malka was as unhappy as the old lady. Nor would Malka tell her that today young wives did not care for these things that had to be starched and ironed, and could not be put in a washing machine, lest they emerge looking like ragged lace. And which young woman today would understand that in being unable to present her precious damask cloth in perfect condition, the old lady would lose her last sense of pride? Oh, a very foolish thing to cry over!

Then there was the matter of pockets. Many an unsteady old soul found it hard to lean on a walking stick with one hand, carry a handbag with the other, and also take hold of a railing going up or down stairs, or when an aching back needed to rest for a minute while walking. Malka soon became expert at opening the seam of a skirt and putting in a deep pocket as in men's trousers; then what was needed could go into the pocket and the bag left at home. The freed hand was a boon and earned her many a blessing.

So many banal details, and we had spoken of a romantic narrative. But wait. Here is something unexpected. A quiet man, coming now and again to visit a relative in the Home, took more notice of Malka than she of him. She was therefore surprised when, one day, he asked her:

"What do you do on Shabbat when you are free?"

Malka would not admit to a stranger that, while the rest from work was welcome, the loneliness of the day was very often unbearable. In her quasi-humorous fashion, she answered him as though his question had been impertinent:

"Sir, I twiddle my toes!"

She turned away immediately, leaving him wondering at such a reply. A week later he again approached, this time with Viennese courtesy:

"Madame, I too twiddle my toes on Shabbat. Would you care to take a walk with me on a Saturday evening? We could then have a coffee somewhere. I would be honored!"

This time she did not turn away. He had addressed her as "Madame." The way she had addressed her employer at the consulate? In all her years in Haifa no one had used the term "Madame" to her – or indeed to anyone. Who had such fine manners here? She was "Malka" to her friends, *"G'veret"* (Mrs.) to others.

Inwardly, she was thinking: "Malka, you're getting on for fifty-five. Have more sense!"

Still. Shabbat was not an easy day to get through on one's own in a small cubby-hole of a room at the top of the Senior Citizens' Home. And the lights of Haifa seen from the Panorama Road form such an exquisite sight; and sitting in a café in the company of a single male – that was something she had not done since – well, never mind since when. Viennese woman that she was, cafés were the acceptable place for meeting friends and relatives; but, popular as she might be, and loved by all who knew her, no one guessed that she might often be alone and lonely. That was the pride that had earned her the nickname "Majestic Malka."

They took many a walk thereafter on a Shabbat evening, along that beautiful road overlooking Haifa, drank many a cup of coffee together. He was not a talkative man, which surprised her; in her opinion, men were anything but shy, generally, but Malka enjoyed telling him about such troubles as the onions, and her unpleasant former job, and she did not forget the Purimspiel, and they had much to laugh about. Above all, Malka was glad to have a friendship of this kind. It was different.

Nor was he too shy to suggest, after many walks and many coffees:

"We are both alone, Malka, let us get married, then we shall not need to go walking when winter comes, we shall have no lonely evenings, no Shabbat toe twiddling."

So he had a sense of humor, too. That suited her. She could have a real home of her own again? She had long since ceased even to dream of such a thing. Oh, but it was tempting! Home! That was a word!

How often had Malka looked in shop windows and seen dishes and silverware that cried out to be bought. For so many years had she eaten off crockery "provided for the servants," and more recently the dull, regulation stuff of the Home, heavy, not easily breakable.

She would be able to indulge her own taste again? Would there be a man coming home after his day's work to be welcomed with the kind of meal that only she could cook? And if she happened to be late from her own job, there would be someone waiting to welcome her?

It did not seem possible, and yet the opportunity had been offered her. She would be able to invite her daughter and son-in-law, there would be a modest kind of family life once more. Her picture of "home," this small, four-lettered word used so casually, this finally ensnared her.

So now the curtain goes up to show this middle-aged couple standing before the Rabbi with two witnesses. There are no guests, there will be no wedding feast, Malka finds that unsuitable. She has put on her "good Viennese suit" – hardly worn since that long ago day when she sat in Haifa port on her suitcase in which it lay. She would have worn it to disembark in Trieste from that ship she never boarded.

The groom, too, has put on a tailored jacket – good Viennese tailoring. He is perhaps a centimeter or so shorter than our Majestic Malka, but under the old trilby hat he found in his closet the difference is not noticeable.

The Rabbi intones the blessings, and suddenly Malka finds tears running down her cheeks. She cannot restrain them. Luckily, the light blue square of voile thrown over her head and face hide the tears.

It is over. Malka is a wife once more. She takes her husband's arm, and they go to the small, one-roomed flat bought with their joint savings. Malka has had the balcony enclosed, so that her husband can have a corner of his own. She has furnished the flat and made it homelike with the bric-a-brac so beloved of Viennese.

Her tears have dried. There is a smile of hope in her eyes.

Some days later her first visitor arrives. It is Fräulein, taught all those years ago not to scratch blisters. She looks around the cosy room with joy, so glad for her old friend, and shakes Reuben's hand with a hearty *"Mazal Tov."* She has brought a small gift, but when she gets up to leave, Malka hands her wordlessly a piece of soft velvet material. Intuitively, Fräulein knows what it is meant for. On her next visit, the velvet has been sewn up into a handsomely embroidered cover for the prayer book. It is placed reverently on the shelf decked with two simple brass candlesticks. Malka's feeling is that she owes the God of Israel a great debt of gratitude. She has a single reservation: that her son should come back.

Life returns to normal. Bride and groom – say, rather, husband and wife – have their early breakfast together and go to their separate jobs. Malka does her daily eight hours with the old and infirm in the Home (see the capital H, signifying something quite other than what it had done in Vered's childhood) and then goes home. Ah me, what a thing that is!

If only it had lasted.

* *
*

Change for Vered, too

For the first time since she arrived in this bare, unlived-in land, Vered found herself living in a town. She rented a room in a large, old-fashioned apartment built around the beginning of this century. Houses were then going up outside the walls of the historic, ancient Jewish City of Jerusalem.

Her room had a high, arched ceiling and small windows set in very thick walls; such walls kept the rooms cool during the long, dry summers. Their thickness formed wide window ledges, and on these Vered placed ornaments, flower pots, photographs in stand-up frames. The arched ceiling appealed to the cultured sense of architecture that had been an integral part of her early education in the long-lost world of Her Old Lady. The room was spacious enough to allow a patrician arrangement of furniture, so that a visitor would be ushered into an airy elegant sitting-room rather than into a "bed-sitter." After the square white house and then the donkey stable, Vered had a sense of satisfaction that had long been a stranger to her.

At night, however, when she liked to read in bed by the light of her tall standing lamp, with music coming softly from the radio on her side-table, the ceiling would thrust strangely shaped shadows across the whitewashed walls. Then she would wonder if she really liked that arched ceiling. Sternly, she admonished herself:

"You have been living in a donkey shed, and now you bother about shadows? For shame!"

Her life had taken a strange route from Stuttgart to Berlin, to the as yet unbuilt village, to the place where her donkey once dwelt, then, via the Panorama Hotel to the revered Holy City. Her landlady, scion of an old family that had lived in Jerusalem for generations, had more than a smattering of German, and the two lonely women conversed in a bookish, musical companionship that left the chicken run and the vegetable plots as the most distant of memories. Vered's enjoyment of her new surroundings was marred only by the gnawing worry for her daughter.

The rent was easily paid from the income on the house she had let out back there, but a job was necessary, as much to occupy her during the long days as for the essentials of daily life. She found one in a small hotel frequented mainly by tourists.

Her employer was a small, round man with a head of thick hair that had once been light brown and now became darker as it grew more gray. As often as he combed it, he would examine his hair with concentration, making a note in his diary to see his hairdresser whenever it needed dyeing again. The manager of a hotel had to make an impressive appearance! He had been thrown out of Europe? Foreign guests would return to their homes with quite a different picture of Jews, he told himself as he stood erect, his hair oiled back, greeting his clients in the entrance hall.

But ensuring the profitability of the hotel was equally important. The expenses were great. The little man's energy was prodigious, his staff as small as possible.

Vered changed sheets, made beds, saw that the rooms were aired, made certain the cleaning woman did her job, kept count of the linen that went to the laundry and of the fresh linen from the closets. She worked willingly and conscientiously, having no difficulty in understanding her employer's Germanic zeal for thoroughness of detail. One can imagine how grateful she was for the couch awaiting her in her own room. She walked home leisurely at the end of her day, actually enjoying the sight of stone and concrete on both sides of the street, more than glad to feel paving instead of sand beneath her feet.

The digging and planting, the chickens and the rest of it – it had left her physically exhausted, without the compensation of arousing a mind that liked to think. This stark city, on the other hand, with its scarcity of flowers and greenery, filled her with a sense of awe. She was moving in history.

Jerusalem has that effect on a developed sensitivity. Vered's very efficiency, however, her intelligent approach to a routine task, was soon observed and taken full advantage of by her hard-pressed little employer who – to be fair – had wages, expenses and heavy taxes to think about, not to mention a family to support.

When the kitchen hand did not slice the tomatoes thinly enough to make up the required portions for the dining room, he would go to the bottom of the staircase and call loudly:

"Vered, Vered, down here, please!"

When a greater number of guests than usual clustered around the Reception desk, each clamoring to be shown to the room ordered weeks ago, he knew only one way to deal with the matter:

"Vered, Vered, down here, please!"

When his own desk was littered with bills and letters which had not been sorted into the neat piles he liked, the call would echo up the stairway:

"Vered, Vered, down here, please!"

He never omitted the "please," priding himself on treating his employees politely.

Inevitably the day came when Vered could hardly walk back to her room. Her feet were burning, her knees threatened to buckle under her. When, at home, she had kicked off her shoes and, unusual for her, left them where they dropped, how fine it was to lie on her couch and do nothing more than gaze up at the arched ceiling. Its patterns bent themselves into geometrically shaped forms across the walls. Where formerly she had found these shadows somewhat disturbing, she now found them almost comforting.

Yes, tired Vered, lie back and watch as the form of whatever passes outside your window changes the shape of the shadow from minute to minute in the dim light. Just now it is more restful than reading. And let the radio remain quiet so that the imperative "Down here, please!" will not send its echo to interfere with the soft music you love. We, too, watch the shadows in your quiet room as we sit in our theater seats. We would not ask you for any activity. The curtain drops on the slumbering woman and rises to find her back at work next day.

She has been trying to fit a bulky pillow into its stiffly starched slip. At that moment the "Vered, Vered, down here, please!" rising from the stairs is suddenly too much. Throwing the unfitted pillow onto the bed, she goes slowly down to confront the little man below:

"Sir, I have changed my name. It is not Vered anymore. From now on I am to be called *'Keren-haphuch-hephtsibah'*."

She made the announcement primly, but in a tone of determination. He was too surprised to do more than look at her questioningly.

"By the time you get to the end of 'haphuch' and it's still not finished," she explained, "you will be too tired to call me."

The small man was beside himself.

"How dare you talk to me like that!" he spluttered. "Go to the office right now, take your wages and go!"

He rued his words even as he uttered them, but he could not take them back. Vered was out of the hotel ten minutes later. There were other jobs.

But a more agreeable event was awaiting her.

As had been expected, a truce was arranged – or maybe it was a cease-fire or whatever euphemism expresses the intervals needed by Israel's enemies to take breath and reorganize before making the next attempt to oust the Jews from their land.

And so the return of the captured soldiers was at hand. A truck was to bring them to the artificial border between the old and the new Jerusalem, where a crowd was gathering. That Vered is among the waiting relatives goes without saying. Naturally, her emotions play havoc with her. Her eyes are fixed on the Mandelbaum Gate, she does not even realize that she is not by herself but in the midst of an excited group.

When Seelchen jumped down from the truck, Vered could hardly breathe. Her lips quivered as her daughter ran into her embrace, but speak she could not.

"It's all right, Ima," the girl assured her, "stop looking so worried, they didn't hurt us at all."

Seelchen continued to chatter until she saw the blood returning to her mother's cheeks:

"They fed us on bread and jam all the time, and plenty of tea. Ima, don't ever give me any jam again! Where are you staying, Ima? We are not going back to the donkey shed! Let us stay here for a few days, yes. Please Ima!"

This brought Vered back to reality. She actually had her Seelchen back. Had the child hated that shed as much as she herself had? They had lived there in quiet good humor, neither making any complaint.

Vered had long forgotten the maxims of Her Old Lady, her life had turned upside down. Nor did she know the English writer, Chesterton, well read as she was, or she might have quoted:

"Fools, for I also had my hour / One far, fierce hour and sweet..." as, indeed, the donkey had – the one that carried Esther Kordovi to and from her hilltop home, as well as the one that afforded two women a residence in their hour of need.

Vered found her voice at last. She launched into an account of her days during Seelchen's absence, and both women laughed heartily at how a change of name got Vered freed from drudgery.

Now plans could be made: The orange grove would again be exporting fruit, there would be income from it... But here she is interrupted:

"No, Ima, we shall sell the house, the grove and all, and get ourselves a place here in Jerusalem. Oh, here comes my friend, Abel. Do you remember him, Ima? He has brought his taxi and will take us – where are you staying?"

Vered has not expected any boy friend, she would rather have had her child to herself right now, but they do need to get home, out of the crowd into her quiet room. She accepted the intrusion silently, getting into the taxi with her daughter, while Abel seated himself behind the steering wheel.

Knowing her mother, Seelchen continued chattering as the car moved off:

"It is my turn to get a job now, and you will stay at home and read and listen to music all the day. Of course, you'll have a meal ready for us when I get home, won't you, Ima? But no jam. Bread and cheese will do, if we can't afford anything else."

This young girl is not intended to be a strand of the particular human plait we are trying to braid here, except insofar as she is Vered's daughter. Having grown up in this country, she is not different from the native-born *Sabras* of Israel; they may be prickly on the outside, often brash and crude, but they are wholesome enough at the core – so long as they do not succumb to the seeming enticements of Americanization which suit neither the culture nor the conditions of our people and their spot on earth.

They now drove to Vered's room where Abel left them. After a few days of rest and chatter, Seelchen found work, and the shadows seemed to vanish. A few weeks later, Seelchen announced her intention of getting married.

"I want a proper home, Ima, and children. You'll be such a lovely grandma and do all the baby-sitting, so I can go on working. Abel earns quite well with his taxi, and my job isn't too bad. Won't you just love having babies on your lap?"

Parks were being laid out in Jerusalem; Vered had a vision of again wheeling babies in their carriages or strollers, enjoying the peacefulness of green grass and seeing flowers even in the stony harshness of this ancient city. She would have liked her daughter to herself for a while longer but, after all, the girl would have to settle down one day.

After a small, modest wedding, Seelchen goes to her own home. And Vered will continue to look up at the arched ceiling, to consider without emotion the strange shapes of the shadows; but still, life is different with a married daughter. There is less loneliness and there is hope.

But whoever claimed that life is an honest grocer, giving full value for what one has paid? As with Esther Kordovi, one dare not expect full measure.

A year or so later, Seelchen, after a difficult pregnancy, gave birth to a still-born child. There will be no baby-sitting for grandma this time.

When Seelchen was fit enough to leave the hospital, Vered felt she could take no more. Her daughter was still young, she had a husband who would care for her and she could yet have children. But Vered again felt that her heart was breaking. It was so unfair. Once more she was on the bus to Haifa for Fräulein's healing company. This time she stayed for many weeks.

* * *

Another change for Malka

In the garden of Fräulein's house, there are two mulberry trees. One bears heavy, juicy berries of great sweetness, while the berries of the second are smaller, darker and rather tart.

Boiled together, the fruit makes a fine, thick jam with a taste and texture that is out of the ordinary. A large container stands on the ground between the trees, as do two ladies, one short and quick in her movements, the other tall and stately, both looking older than their years. Their present task is to pick the fruit. They eat while they pick, and the bright red juice runs down their faces, coloring their chins and turning their fingers purple. They look at each other and burst into laughter. It is long since either of them has laughed so heartily.

"Our Fräulein will make a good confiture from this," says Vered, "and I'll take some home, even if my Seelchen won't eat it."

Malka suggests they had better go in and wash their faces before anyone sees them. The container is just about full, and both women are tired. Inside the house, their hands and faces shining clean, they sit down to a cup of coffee, prattling over this and that, as if they had known each other all their lives, although it is only a week or so since they first met.

How have our strands come together like this, meeting for the first time, although both have known their hostess these many years?

Vered, we know, is here to regain a measure of tranquillity after her daughter's misfortune. But Malka? Had she not got married? Had she not a small, cosy home of her own in Haifa?

What then has happened? Malka's husband, Reuben, had "been through the mill" before arriving in Haifa some time after the war. He had lost his family; he had known the type of "living" that survival in concentration camp demanded. Integration in Israel had also not been easy: The damp summer heat was uncomfortable, the new language was difficult, but he had to learn it to get work; finding suitable work and an affordable style of life was also quite an effort. Even the routine of getting up at a certain hour in the morning to be at his workplace punctually – even this was burdensome. When he had dreamt, during that abhorrent period – if he had ever been able to dream – he had dreamt of "being free." And now he was free – but somehow, he had never understood what being "free" would imply.

Now, after his marriage, he soon perceived that he was being given – on a silver platter, so to speak – all the elements of the real, good life. His tall, fine-looking wife cooked marvelously. She kept the little flat scrupulously clean and tidy, she had even in that small area provided him with a corner of his own. And she made few demands on him, other than expecting him to pay some of the household bills and an occasional evening out.

Of his own accord, he decided one day that "enough was enough." He had the opportunity to retire from work and live in ease – and live in ease he would. He said not a word of this to his wife, except to mention that he did not need to be in his office as early as hitherto.

A period of Festivals was coming up, and Malka obtained permission to leave her work earlier than usual for a week or two. She was planning on having "real" Festival days, with traditional dishes, company and family. It would be the first time she could do this since she had come to the country.

It was an unexpected shock to find her Reuben lying contentedly on his couch, a cigar in his mouth filling the room with smoke and the radio at full blast. Malka's first thought, naturally, was womanly: "Are you ill? Is anything wrong?"

He was too cowardly then to admit to the truth. It was good to be made a fuss of, even though she opened all the windows to let clean air into the room. Sternly, she took the cigar from him and threw it into the garbage can.

"That will harm your lungs," she admonished, "and mine, too; I cannot breathe in such air."

Still, he said nothing, just murmured weakly:

"What do you want, Malka? I'm not disturbing you."

She gave him a sharp look. Working with the old and the infirm, she had learned to recognize malingering for the sake of a little extra care. She did not wish to cloud her mind now with suspicion, and suggested it would do him good to take a walk in the fresh air. He could do some shopping for her on the way, there were some ingredients she needed for the Festivals.

For the next few days she made a point of coming home earlier than he would expect, and always the same scene awaited her: He lay there smoking a fine cigar, listening to music.

Malka was too great-souled a woman to begrudge this new husband the ease he appeared to be so urgently in need of; but as the days became weeks, she could not entirely banish the suspicion. She went to his place of work, where the truth was disclosed: He had given in his resignation of his own accord, he had not been made redundant.

She neither ranted nor shouted. In her deep Viennese voice, this time with no trace of a caress in her tone, she told him:

"No, *mein Herr*, I shall not work my feet off all day with my truly infirm, lonely old inmates, so that you can lie here in peace and smoke. Can you find anyone in this country whose life has run blandly along without any hardships?

"We shall have to go to the Rabbi again. You will find yourself somewhere to live, and you will give me a *get*, a divorce!"

Reuben knew she was inexorable. He had not been sensible, he told himself.

No tears rolled down her face this time. She held herself proudly at the Rabbinate, our true, majestic Malka. The little flat was sold, the proceeds equally divided; the beloved knickknacks were packed away with her new dishes and silverware, and she returned to her cubbyhole at the top of the Senior Citizens' Home. She was as kind to her old folk as formerly, made as many humorous comments as she always had done, and let no one suffer from the pain inside herself.

But one day she lost her footing on the narrow, spiral staircase. She was a heavy woman, her legs were broken in many parts. The next three months were spent in hospital. It is rather silly to blame one's fate. The Almighty works in His own way. For a few days after each major operation, Malka lay as if in a coma, with no idea of anything happening around her. She did not know that her daughter had come from Tel Aviv to sit at her bedside, nor had she any idea that sitting next to her daughter there was also a man, a gaunt creature, skin stretched taut over his bones, and not an ounce of flesh on him. But if one examined him carefully, one could see he was as tall as Malka and had her very features. The relationship could not be mistaken.

Once he turned to the nurse who had come to give Malka an injection, asking: "Is she a difficult patient, nurse?"

"Difficult?" repeated the nurse, while brother and sister smiled at each other, remembering the autocratic mother of "the old days in Vienna."

"She is an angel," declared the nurse, and Malka woke up as the needle entered her vein.

"I am going to the angels?" she asked sleepily, then turned her head with a sudden widening of her eyes. She seemed to have heard a familiar voice. And her son, bending to kiss her, said also in the semi-humorous Viennese tone:

"Mama, you have changed. The nurse says you are angelic!"

Not every scene should be described and watched. Her son had been in and out of the most horrible concentration camps. One way or another, he had kept himself alive, skeleton as he looked.

Brother and sister visited their mother daily, but when she was allowed to go home, there was no real home. Her son was in a transit camp, she did not want to go to Tel Aviv, and in any case her daughter had to go to work daily and could not look after her, nor could she manage that spiral staircase to her old cubby hole.

Fräulein came to the rescue. Malka and Vered together in her home – it was ideal. Nothing but close, true friendship could develop between two such fine women. Vered had to return to Jerusalem one day, but came back to visit often enough. She did get grandchildren, could take them out in their carriages, a dream come true. And Malka, too, recovered sufficiently to walk with a cane. She returned to the Home, this time as an inmate; her son married eventually, and she, too, had a grandchild from each of her children.

* *
*

Ora in an unpleasant scene

One of our strands has gone to her final rest, and the others are, for the moment at least, at their ease. It would be fine to stop there and let the curtain down.

But the world is a globe that turns. In the nature of things, it must at some point return to a spot of past familiarity. The generation of that time will, hopefully, have regained a sense of justice and of humanity, and will want to know: What exactly did happen? How did it come to pass? Why?

Perhaps there are no adequate answers. But so far as it lies in one's power, one has a duty to record what evidence one has. History has known a great many wars, but this particular one, the Nazi war, destroyed too much of the good that lies at the core of human nature. Bitterness and hatred are in themselves destructive, whether of victims, whether of perpetrators. There is no sense or logic in expecting that period to have produced a trump card for a better future.

You have no alternative, Ora, you are obliged, indeed obligated, to recall memories even if they disturb what inner peace you have attained, even after half a century. You may wonder what right one has to probe like this. But as much knowledge as possible must be made available, however long it may take until a craving for understanding awakens.

There is no option, Ora, tell on! She does:

"Did I mention that I was transferred to Lindenfels? What I saw there shocked me more than anything else, so now and again I went to Lampertheim to visit my old group there. They crowded around me, gave me such a warm welcome; I sensed an atmosphere of great excitement. You can't imagine how they all talked at once with an enthusiasm I had never felt among that apathetic lot of young people."

"Did they have some special news for you?"

"Of course. There was an older chap among them, the type that likes to take on the role of leadership, that always knows the best way to do things. He had promised that by means of the 'illegal *Aliyah* B,' he would take them all out of this hated farm and its labor and get them to Palestine; they had only to put their trust in him.

"They were too glad to do so. It was the promise they had been waiting for."

Ora shakes her head: "They had been through so much, they were so unnaturally mature for their years – and yet so naive. Well, this self-appointed leader set up a fund. Each would contribute whatever he or she could. They may have gotten some pocket money for their work, such as it was, I wouldn't know. But they were liberally supplied with cigarettes, and these were of greater worth than money.

"It was quite natural, I suppose," says Ora thoughtfully, "that a savage world regressed to the barter system of ancient times. For a certain number of cigarettes one could squeeze out of the Germans whatever one desired; cigarettes were a real source of private revenue. This leader chap, of course, collected from the group as much as he could – and they gave it to him unquestioningly. I was so shocked!"

Today, Ora is surprised that after everything she had seen, she could yet have been shocked. When this leader was away for a few hours, she got a group together and advised them to keep exact accounts. She showed them precisely how everything should be registered, how to note down both the contributions and the expenditure. Thus the fund would be correctly organized.

The group liked Ora. She had been good to them, but she was not part of their raw world where "survival at all costs" was the name of the game. Bookkeeping was not on their program. Getting away from Europe to Palestine was. They had no other goal.

Ora was powerless to prevent what would have been obvious to anyone from a normal world. On her next visit, the group had vanished. Rumor had it that their "leader" had taken them to Paris on the way to Marseilles and thence to Palestine.

But in Paris he disappeared. The group was left stranded with hardly a penny among the lot. Somehow or other, they straggled back to Lampertheim, where they remained until the State of Israel was proclaimed. Had it not been, had the Yishuv leaders not had the guts to establish the State, utter despair, complete hopelessness would have added Heaven knows how many to the six million already at rest from the agony the world had inflicted.

"I met this 'leader' once in Tel Aviv," says Ora. "I recognized him immediately. I stopped and looked him straight in the eye. But then I walked on. Should I have stood and shouted: 'You took all that they had and then abandoned them?' and then called him names? He knew what he had done. Why blame him, in fact? The whole world with its governments, its parliaments and politicians, its military industries and its glib talk of 'democracy' – if the world had anything like a collective conscience, it should still today be suffering the torments of the damned. But who cares?"

The air of depression in the room is like a fog. No cups of tea can dilute its thickness. The voice of the interviewer breaks the few minutes of silence:

"That is why I am so hard on you, forcing you to rake up these memories. The dead do not suffer. But those who had to find their way, stumbling blindly, distraught, taking wrong or crooked paths – did they play no role in the forming of our post-war world?"

Now Ora smiles, if somewhat wryly: "I told you, there were and are no ideals. From their past, they could only have learned that it is each for himself. You cannot turn the clock back and teach it ethics as if from the letter A. And then, did you yourself not say that each one of us is no more significant than – "

"– a strand of hair. I know. And the wind blows the strands in all directions. But tell me, how did you react when you learned about that bedraggled lot being back in Lampertheim?"

"How should I have reacted? Inside myself I was shouting and screaming, but if I had screamed aloud out in the middle of the camp, who would have been helped? Probably they would have thought me mad and locked me up."

She is perhaps right. "Go on, what happened next?"

"I was sent to Lindenfels for the summer; I must have told you that. And then the few hundred children there were sent to Dornstadt, and I was instructed to take care of them there. So I went to Dornstadt. That was even more terrible. You don't want to hear about that."

"No, I don't *want* to, but if there is something to be told, my wanting or not has nothing to do with it!"

"Don't say I didn't warn you. The children there were of all ages, from pre-school to around fifteen. That winter of 1946-1947 was particularly severe and, believe it or not, most of the smaller ones went around barefoot; they had neither shoes nor socks, their little feet were blue from cold. The authorities had not yet gotten around to that problem, there were too many problems to be dealt with."

"Please, continue."

"During the journey, the children had been looked after by a number of adults who remained in Dornstadt ostensibly to help care for their charges. I imagine that accompanying the children from Poland to Germany was a means of getting themselves out of Poland; for all these adults (we called them 'refugees') had endured the bitterness of life in Nazism, either in concentration camps or as partisans fighting from the 'shelter' of the thick, dark forests. They were just as indifferent to working in Dornstadt as my DPs had been to learn farming in Lampertheim. It was thought to brighten up this children's camp by planting flower gardens, putting down grass and so on. But those adult refugees were lethargic to any idea of work.

"Anyway, the problem of keeping the toddlers a bit warmer had to be dealt with, and we set up a committee in a very formal, democratic way. 'Those above,' making decisions in their official quarters, thought that making the refugees members of a committee, able to voice their opinions and vote on decisions, would help the refugees to regain a measure of self-respect."

Ora's voice expresses little respect for that notion. She goes on: "It was decided to have socks knitted for the smallest of the children – they had first claim to care. A quantity of wool and knitting needles was procured, and I was made responsible for seeing that the task was carried out."

(Does the ghost of Esther Kordovi arise? She, too, had knitted to keep young soldiers warm on that cold hilltop near Safed. The flesh prickles – at the similarity and at the difference.)

"Part of the wool was handed to those of the 'committee' prepared to see that the knitting was done. The rest was locked away for later distribution when the first batch was to be delivered. But someone must have taken note of where I had placed the wool and the key to the locker.

"Oh, how I looked forward to seeing some of those blue little feet finally encased in woolen socks. But when I opened the locker to take out the second batch of wool in preparation for distribution, it was empty. The wool had vanished."

Ora is silent again. One becomes impatient. This knitting was a good idea. What could have gone wrong? Tell and have done with it!

But the very air in the room is thick with the fog of despair. No cups of tea can soothe. She is urged on:

"So what did happen?"

And heavily Ora reveals:

"I found no wool, but I thought the knitting had been done more quickly. So I went around hoping to collect the socks or booties. Of course, there were none. You want to know what happened? The committee members, men and women, all older and stronger than our camp inmates, they were strutting around, quite unashamed, wearing warm sweaters and shawls made of our wool. Apparently they had offered some small payment of cigarettes or chocolate to the German peasant women of the neighborhood to knit for them."

What, indeed, can one say? How terribly, how deeply, how wickedly had those "refugees" been made to suffer till they lost all sense of consideration, all feeling for anyone other than their separate selves? On whom shall one pass judgment?

"Yes," agrees Ora in a voice trying, fifty years later, not to get worked up, "it was cold, they were cold, we were all cold, the tiny children were cold, very cold. Do you have a word in your innumerable lexicons," she asked her friend, busy taking notes, "that can adequately express how simple human beings were deliberately made to be soulless because they happened to be Jews?"

There are no facile phrases with which to respond. An attempt is made to ease the heavy atmosphere: "What about food? Did everyone in the camp get enough to eat? The little ones, too?"

"Oh, yes, the menu was dull but plentiful. Bread and potatoes were ample for all. The survivors did not suffer from hunger anymore."

And that, for now, will have to suffice for a handsbreadth of reassurance. What is surprising, perhaps, is Ora having built her life in Israel. When her term of duty was over, she returned to London, studied at the university and could have had a satisfying academic career. Yet, five or six years later, we meet her in Jerusalem, knowing no one, not even her way around town to find her rented room.

Religion had no part in her life and, knowledgeable as she was, understanding of Jewish culture and philosophy formed no part of her erudition.

But it is not really so puzzling. One may guess that in Israel she could rid herself of the heavy "sack" that had burdened her adolescence. In Israel she was a person among her own kind. There was no sack to carry.

She may even have needed to see for herself what kind of country was emerging – remembering the human material she had known during its worst moment. She had seen for herself the heavy weight of their "sack." From childhood in her own home she had been aware of the superstitions that – out of calamities befalling only Jews – had evolved in hamlets and ghettoes across the world, distant, isolated, yet always related by their Jewishness. From the example of her parents she had seen the unwavering trust of the faithful, although this had been an enigma to her. From her own experience in her young adulthood she had seen the dilemma of the homeless nation, the enforced wandering, the cruel displacement and – yes, the distorted way of living which the world in its hatred or shoulder-shrugging apathy so thoroughly taught the victims it had ensnared.

Ora came late to Israel. But she is no less part of the human plait braided by the single strands blown here long before the State of Israel made them citizens of their own home.

* * *

Our strands are braided, the curtain drops

Figuratively speaking, it is Shabbat. The simple souls we have gotten to know in these pages deserve now to take their rest. Like their counterparts all over Israel, they gave of themselves as they could to the stupendous making of a homeland for this memory-ridden nation of Jews. The word "heroism" evokes deeds of "derring-do" – to which none of our *dramatis personae* would lay claim. But unique memories burden each of them, and when, alone, they sit back and reminisce, their reaction to the entirety of their separate lives is one and the same. As if with one voice, the exclamation is heard:

"What have we not seen in our single lifetime?"

Near the beginning of this narrative, we saw an old lady in an armchair, looking back, making an attempt to "attain some comprehension from the distance of time." As are the others, she is aware of a vague feeling of dissatisfaction. It bothers her, as it does the others. It requires analysis.

A real country has grown out of the sand, the boulders, the thorns and the thistles. The rough ground has been tamed. There are roads, proper roads that one can walk on without sinking into the sand or getting one's ankles scratched by the thorns along a dirt track. The streets have names, they are lined with houses, shops, offices, the very pavements are full of parked cars. It has such a prosperous appearance, this brand-new little Israel, so begrudged by its old-established neighbors.

The arid soil has been made fruitful; many of the once harsh, barren hilltops, untouched, untrodden since the start of the Common Era, are now lush with trees and hedges and flowering shrubs. The earth gives forth its produce as if with joy and gratitude for the loving hands that have, at last, tended it. The houses are full of life. One hears the laughter of children at play, the hum of talk and work behind the walls of schools, factories, warehouses – the ordinary sounds of life anywhere in the world. The few hundred thousand of the thirties and forties have grown to millions.

The language itself, for so long restricted to the "Holy Tongue" of study and prayer, is aglow with lively development, even to its slang! Nor are there any capital letters in Hebrew, not for words that begin sentences, or for names, not even for that highly important "I."

But there are a few letters that change their shape when they end a word, and in this there may be something symbolic, meaningful for the vague dissatisfaction that afflicts our old ladies. Finality changes the shape of things.

The three afflictions of Malka's early days have long been conquered. But they have been replaced by two far worse afflictions. They have no strange-sounding names, nor should they be Latinized into frightening medical terms. For they are purely human, developed somehow or other by ordinary mortals.

The one affliction is the harsh loneliness of old age. From the moment of its rebirth, the Land of Israel has been a country for the young. Like Othello, the old are dispensable, they have done theirs.

So each of our "non-heroines" sits alone in her room. There is no way to change that. A weekday may be gotten through until dusk, but what does one do with long evenings when old folk dislike going out alone? Yes, there are indeed Senior Citizens' Homes – for those with money.

And what about Shabbat? The second generation offspring belong to the "too busy" group, all too busy. And Shabbat is the one day when they can relax. Who would deprive them of that? The question brings us to the second "affliction" of our times: the near-failure to build up a Jewish nation on the basis of its own profound ethical culture. For we have been placed in cells, each cell inimical to the others. Each cell labeled and each intolerant of the others.

Esther Kordovi had an inkling of such a future when she tried, all those years back, to explain life here in that letter to her daughter. She had understood the tendency to the divisiveness but had not dreamt it would become such a significant factor in Israeli life. The phenomenon might also have been inferred by anyone listening to the prattle in the café between Malka and her young friend. It is not surprising that our veterans feel the pain of the divisiveness. Old folk, they know, are considered "not with it"; young people will not listen to the opinion that, interesting and "democratic" as all this diversity may be, it is yet simply silly: Its only outcome can be the weakening of a people whose greatest need is strength.

But what is the use of so much deliberating? They sit in their armchairs, these old friends of ours, each one alone; Malka in the small room allotted to her in the Senior Citizens' Home after her accident. Vered on her couch under the arched ceiling with its shadows. The one-time governess in her room reads as long as the light and her failing eyesight allow her. Ora in her house is restless, getting up, walking about, sitting down again, switching on the TV – oh, awful desecration of the Day of Rest – and a rather cynical notion is in the minds of all four: Some people are too busy being holy to remember lonely old relatives, while others are too occupied with their relaxations and diversions and the society that never mixes friends with family. In any case, a lonely old widow is an encumbrance, it is easier not to bring her to mind.

As with Ora, long effort, unkind memories and the creeping years cause any person to become restless, aimless. These old ladies of ours – be they the four plaited into one (and the art of the cinema would find it simple to superimpose face on face, so that one face serves for all four) – ask themselves a hundred times a day, and too often during the long, hateful night: "Why? Why am I become as if non-existent? Why? Why?"

In the silence that shrieks from the walls, the repetition echoes till it begins to sound like the Yiddish *"Weh!"* (Woe!); this is intolerable, self-pity must not be allowed. After all, her (their) life has been full and useful.

With a heavy movement, leaning on the arm of the chair for support, the old body is freed; she stands erect. Just stands. There is nowhere to go, nothing to do on Shabbat. She can pace up and down in her room. Back and forth, so many meters each way. She counts them. When she has paced a hundred meters, she (they) can sit down again.

Were there actually men of science who used their laboratories and their learning in the attempt to prolong life?

"Lord, what fools these mortals be!" Eternally meaningful quotation.

"One must be fair," comes the admonishment, "you have forgotten those early days when one saw so few elderly people, and mostly the young were here. Few of those youngsters grew to maturity in the secure atmosphere of family *Yiddishkeit*. And what of those who had kept themselves alive by any and all possible means? What should today's young population have inherited from all this? What kind of conduct?"

The word "secure" has its own emphasis, it is too disturbing, too reminiscent of the dire meaning that "insecurity" holds for Jews.

Again our old lady (or ladies) will get up and walk around the room. But a voice is heard. A figure has detached itself from the others.

It is Ora. She has not completed her telling of life in the DP camps. She might just have been recollecting for some minutes:

"Certainly they were no longer hungry, neither the children, nor the adults. It was the Germans who were hungry, starving almost as they well deserved to be. I might have felt sorry for them at first, but the more I saw of what they had done to our people, the less I got to bother myself about the Germans. All my sense of pity, sorrow, sympathy – call it what you will – was focused on our Jewish survivors, no matter how they behaved. It was all nothing compared with what had been done to them.

"As I told you, there were still some DPs in a fair state of mind and health, and these were given special jobs. They were learning the feeling of responsibility by working with their weaker fellows, like my driver – I love the way you called him my 'chauffeur' –

"Well, among these was a young doctor. He had barely had time to practice his profession, he had just finished his studies when the Nazis came to power. He had been through the concentration camps, he had lost his entire family, anything he had ever possessed. But he had a stubborn intensity, hard to explain. He had not only kept his knowledge intact, but he had kept the clarity of his soul. Does that phrase sound extravagant? I can describe it in no other way. Despite all his suffering, his soul remained crystal pure.

"So, as I said, it was the Germans who went hungry. When the loaves of bread were delivered to us in the mornings, the local peasant women would watch, furtively crouching behind a tree or hedge. Once one of these women crept up and swiftly took a loaf of bread. She hid it under her apron and turned to run. But she had been noticed. The person in charge of our unit of the Relief Agency ran after her, screaming as one possessed:

"'Put that back! Put that loaf back where it was, you rotten Nazi, you Nazi thief!'

"Then the Jewish doctor, who had been standing near the van, approached the angry woman and spoke to her so softly, so gently:

"'See,' he told her, 'she is hungry. Let her keep the loaf.'"

* *
*

P.S. Our oldsters have gone to their eternal rest; surely there is no loneliness for them in the "World of Eternal Life." Only Ora is still with us, she who told of her experience in the DP camps. It was a painful task. Thank you, Ora; in telling it you have done more than you realize!